The Mind of Man

The Mind of Man

Models of Human Understanding

Anthony J. Sanford

YALE UNIVERSITY PRESS
NEW HAVEN AND LONDON

First published in the United States in 1987 by
YALE UNIVERSITY PRESS

© Anthony J. Sanford, 1987

Printed in Great Britain

Library of Congress catalog card number: 86–51571
International standard book number: 0 300 03960 3

This book is dedicated to my daughter Bridget

Contents

Figures

Preface

In the late winter of 1983, I gave a short series of Gifford Lectures at the University of Glasgow. These public lectures, founded in the last century, are in Natural Theology. At first, while being honoured, I was equally bemused. The reason for my bemusement was straightforward. What could a cognitive psychologist have to say about natural theology?

A little investigation made me feel rather easier about the matter. The Gifford Lectures have been used as a forum for the exposition of science as well as for more plainly theological topics, encompassing the work of Eddington on the nature of the physical world, and Sherrington on a physiologist's view of man's nature, as well as Barth and Marcel.[1] These scientific expositions were both popular discussions of the subject matter and contributions to the way we understand ourselves and the universe about us. There is little doubt that these expositions of science put a certain perspective on how relationships between man and the universe might be conceived. My own contribution concerned the way in which cognitive psychologists conceive of human understanding itself, which is what the present volume is about.

The present work is a revision and extension of my original lectures, previously published in a limited edition.[2] As was the case with the lectures, the theme is the psychological approach to how human beings understand things, looked at from my own point of view. In particular, I was concerned with what might be said about the basis of understanding and the nature of misunderstanding. This is not only an area

of research in which I am personally interested, it is related
to a point made by Lord Gifford. Writing of his reasons for
instituting the lecture series, he said:

I have been for many years deeply and firmly convinced that the true
knowledge of God ... the true and felt knowledge (not mere nominal
knowledge) of the relations of man and the universe to Him ... is the
means of man's highest well-being and the security of his upward progress
...[3]

That which caught my attention in this passage was the
contrast between true and felt knowledge and the mere
nominal. It seemed to me to reflect a clear philosophy of
education, and one which invites psychological comment.
What is learned should not be simply recountable, but
should be intuitively felt. This is presumably what we mean
when we say that someone has a 'good feel' for something.

It is certainly the case that just feeling sure about something does not necessarily mean that one is either correct or
justified in being confident about it. Whenever we turn to
what people believe or hold to be true, there is potential
room for error. The psychology of understanding is as much
concerned with explaining false impressions as it is concerned with the acquisition of knowledge. Much of this book
is about these issues.

The scientific study of understanding and intuition leads
not only to a better understanding of ourselves, but reminds
us of the distinction between knowledge and certainty, so
vigorously championed by the late Jacob Bronowski.[4]
Knowledge may change, and may be readily acknowledged
as incomplete, but feelings of certainty have the unfortunate
property of closing the mind. The contrast may perhaps be
indicated by the distinction between the regular interpretation of the phrase 'I know my mind', and what it should
mean. It normally means that I am set on a course of action,
or set in attitude—basically immovable, of course. What it
should mean is that I understand myself, even if that understanding means the appreciation of uncertainty, doubt and
the possibility of error.

This book is not a textbook. It is a collection of perspectives on human understanding written from the point of view

of my own interests. The assertions made are, of course, not without foundation. Indeed, much of what I have to say may be considered by some colleagues as very much state of the art. The chapter notes contain references to the relevant technical sources. Although this method of citing references is not the most convenient for the academic, it is best for the lay reader for whom the book is intended.

My own perspective is firmly rooted in the new discipline of cognitive science, which is an interdisciplinary subject using insights from linguistics, philosophy, computing science and engineering, as well as from psychology. Such an amalgam is believed by many to be necessary if we are to achieve a realistic understanding of human mentality.

I would like to thank the Gifford Committee for inviting me to give the lectures on which this volume is based. I would also like to acknowledge support from the ESRC and SERC who funded the research drawn upon in Chapter 2. Special thanks are due to those colleagues who discussed these matters with me, especially my close colleague Simon Garrod with whom I work on language understanding, and to Dennis Hilton with whom I had timely discussions about attribution theory. Without the support and cheerfully given help of Linda Moxey, the book may never have been completed.

CHAPTER 1

Mental Process

When one thinks about how an everyday mechanical device works, with a little exposure one finds it a relatively easy matter. Thus when a pedal of a bicycle is pressed down, a cog is turned because the arm of the pedal rotates. The teeth of the cog push the chain forward. The chain pushes the rear cog, which rotates, and so the rear wheel rotates which causes the bicycle to move. It is no problem to see a clear and substantial connection between the pedal motion and the bicycle motion. A little investigation and we see how a pump works, how a steam engine works, and so on. Some knowledge of physiology and biochemistry, and one can understand in terms of concrete observables how light falling on the retina of the eye causes a light-sensitive cell to send an electrochemical pulse to an adjacent nerve, itself electrochemically sensitive, so that ultimately light causes activity in cells in the brain. Although there is some technical difficulty in observing and measuring the important features of nerves and nerve bundles, it is not at all difficult to appreciate the physical events which lead, mechanically, from light to brain activity.

The compelling concreteness of these physical event sequences rests upon the observability of the components of the brain. Of course, when one enters the realm of modern physics, it is necessary to leave all of this concreteness behind, for normal, concrete, substantial things have little place in modern theoretical physics. As Eddington pointed out, it is just this which makes modern physics difficult to understand.[1] The point I have to make is related but

1

different. It is difficult to think about mental states and events because they cannot be directly observed, and because in no way are they graspable, physical things.

There is a somewhat misleading point of view that one's own experience provides a sufficient understanding of mental life for scientific purposes. Indeed, early in the history of experimental psychology, the main method for studying cognition was *introspection*. By observing one's own mind, the argument went, one could say how one carried out cognitive activities. Certainly, this sometimes appears to be the case. Quickly say which letter of the alphabet comes before 'P'. Before 'U'. Most people find that they are reciting little bits of the alphabet in their heads to find the answer. This is indeed a clue to an important part of the mental operations which go on in the face of this task.[2] Another example is the following task: How many windows were there in the last house in which you lived? As Shepard has pointed out, most people have an impression of mentally 'looking around the house' and counting the windows.[3]

Yet introspection failed to be a good technique for the elucidation of mental processes in general. There are two simple reasons for this. First, so many things which we can do seem to be quite unrelated to conscious experience. Someone asks you your name. You do not know how you retrieve it, yet obviously there is some *process* by which the retrieval occurs. In the same way, when someone speaks to you, you understand what they say, but you do not know how you came to understand. Yet somehow processes take place in which words are picked out from the jumble of sound waves which reach your ears, in-built knowledge of syntax and semantics gives it meaning, and the significance of the message comes to be appreciated. Clearly, introspection is not of much use here, but it is undeniable that understanding language is as much a part of mental life as is thinking.

As if these arguments were not enough, it is also the case that introspective data are notoriously difficult to evaluate. Because it is private to the experiencer, an experience may be difficult to convey in words to somebody else. Many early introspective protocols were very confusing to read and, even worse, the kinds of introspection reported tended to conform to the theoretical categories used in different laboratories.[4] Clearly, what was needed was both a change in experimental method and a different (non-subjective) theoretical framework to describe mental life.

PROCESS-MODELS

The approach to cognitive theorising which has proved the most fertile emerged over the past thirty years, although it has antecedents which go back centuries.[5] The requirement is for a description of processes in terms which do not necessarily include consciousness, since so many processes are necessarily non-conscious.

The *information processing approach* usually embodies the assumption that what we might term mental activity takes place in the brain, and that any task we perform, any decision we make, is carried out by the operation of brain physiology. Of course, in practice very little is known about the precise way in which many functions are carried out in the brain. But this is not an insurmountable stumbling-block. We can assume that *data* are *stored in memory*, that stored information is used as necessary by some control mechanism in the brain, that representations of problems we are trying to solve are stored temporarily in the brain, and so on. The psychologists' problem is then to say what factors influence how particular information is stored, at which stage in processing certain sorts of information are retrieved and used during processing, the kinds of factor that limit the ease with which a problem can be solved. What most theoretically-oriented cognitive psychologists do is to try to discover the essential form of the chains of events which take place during the performance of cognitive activities. On this view, the brain is viewed as an information processing system in which data can be stored and retrieved, and operated upon.

An important analogy can be drawn between this conception of mental activity and the nature of a computer program. Computer programs simply operate on data stored in computer memory, and this is taken by many cognitive psychologists as being an ideal metaphor for mental activity.

To get the flavour, consider the simple task of determining how people of different ages perform arithmetic tasks like 4 + 5 = ?. If one has *learned* all the answers for digit addition, then the basic data one has could be thought of as being in the form 1 + 3 = 4, 2 + 4 = 8, etc. The unconscious procedures used would reduce to something like 'find the pattern 2 + 4 in memory'. When this pattern is found in memory, the answer will be found. However, if all one could do is count, (i.e. only a counting procedure is stored in memory), then the answer could not be retrieved by this simple pattern-matching process. Rather, 2 + 4 would be interpreted as 'find 2 in the number sequence, count four along from the number, and that is the answer'. These two procedures are very different, and so are the underlying data in memory. In terms of modelling the process, it is an easy matter to set up each account as a computer program. Both versions give the same answers, but in different ways. In fact, these two versions of the process predict rather different patterns for the time that it would take people to perform arithmetic tasks of this simple sort. Thus, as it stands, the 'direct answer' model makes no particular predictions concerning how long it would take to give a particular answer. All should be answered in about the same time. In contrast, the 'addition' account suggests that greater response times would be expected where more counting was involved. For instance, 2 + 4 might take two steps (4, 5,6,) whereas 5 + 4 must take at least four steps (5, 6,7,8,9). In fact, rather detailed models of this type have been developed for child and adult addition.[6] Note that although counting is normally a conscious process, the same type of argument applies whether consciousness enters into it or not. Detailed models of how people carry out 'mental work' are known as *process models*. In the present book, one of our main concerns is the use of process models to understand understanding itself.

Process models have been developed for aspects of memory, perception, problem-solving, language production, speech perception—a whole spectrum of mental activity. Yet step-by-step process models are not and cannot be the whole concern of information-processing theories. It is necessary to make assumptions about the *functional components* of an information processing system.

FUNCTIONAL COMPONENTS

Functional components are in effect the bits and pieces which make up the system in which information processing takes place. Consider a simple task like 'add up the first four digits of the digit sequence'. You have to be able to retrieve from memory the fact that they are 1, 2, 3, 4. Then, as they are added, the result of each sub-addition has to be kept in memory temporarily before the next sub-addition takes place (i.e. $1 + 2 = 3$; $3 + 3 = 6$; $6 + 4 = 10$). From a functional components point of view, such a process model requires: (a) a permanent memory, in which the original string is kept; and (b) a temporary memory in which the result of each sub-addition is kept. It is a convenient analogy to think of memory as data kept in some *place* in the brain, so one speaks of permanent memory *stores*, for instance. In addition to memory stores, there has to be some analogical *place* where the operations of the task itself take place. This is usually referred to as *working memory*, since while the task itself is being carried out, there are various things which have to be temporarily recorded. For instance, for the process model described above to work properly, one has to assume some sort of updatable memory which records where the sub-addition processes have reached. In the first instance, having worked out $1 + 2 = 3$, the system has to have access to the fact that the process has reached a point where the *next* digit to be added on is 3, and after that 4. Because of the changing nature of these sort of data, it is only stored in a temporary way.

Ignoring the considerable experimental and theoretical history of research into the functional components of memory, it is quite fair to generalise upon the main aspects of current conceptions.[7] The first component is long-term memory. This can be thought of as a library of information:

everything we know, believe, everything we can do, every skill we have, is stored here. The sub-components of this are the subject of much investigation and theorising, and some aspects of long-term memory structure inevitably enters our discussion later on. Its main properties are that there appears to be no limit to the amount of data which can be stored in it, and although it may sometimes be difficult to find something in it (as in a library) there is very little evidence that anything is ever lost from it. But perhaps the most remarkable aspect of long-term memory is the ease with which information can be retrieved from it, despite its enormity. One can recognise faces, retrieve the meanings of words, retrieve whole episodes from our lives, recall masses of factual data when required to. Of course, sometimes retrieval will fail, but by and large, retrieval is adequately accurate and astonishingly fast. Given that there is no computer system that can respond so rapidly from such a great database, it is small wonder that much technical research is aimed at unravelling just how human memory is organised. Since it will be argued that much of our understanding is dependent upon getting to the appropriate data in long-term memory, the rapid-access property is arguably central to both the efficiency of human understanding, and to some of the things that can go wrong with it.

In complete contrast to the astonishing efficiency and storage capacity of long-term memory are the memory stores associated with actually carrying out work with data which are retrieved. The idea of a short-term store results from observations like the difficulty one has in remembering more than about six or seven unrelated items of information, such as words or digits. And even if you can remember XOVBNDR, you are unlikely to remember it for very long without continually rehearsing it to yourself. A good practical illustration of the limit of this kind of memory is found in copying numbers from one page to another. It is very difficult to transfer more than about five at a time, and the usual rate is three at a time.[8]

There is a further essential component required for executing most tasks, and that is a place where the operations on the data are actually carried out. There is at least some evidence for a limited capacity functional component which is used in many situations, and it has been variously termed 'functional memory' (in a different sense from ours), 'workspace memory', 'working memory', and 'executive'. Although such a functional component has to be assumed for many tasks, the precise properties of such a working memory are somewhat dependent on the sort of task being carried out. However, it does have the property of being limited in capacity—i.e. not many operations can occur in it at the same time without some breakdown in performance. For instance, if one is playing chess or some similarly complex game and trying to plan ahead, the amount of look-ahead one can manage is limited by working memory.

Current research is much concerned with the nature of working memory, and is undeniably complex. For our purposes the most important aspect of the idea is that because of such a limitation, there is a severe constraint on the kinds of ways in which people can think, solve problems and understand.[9]

The information processing approach thus stresses two things: the *process model* which describes how a task is performed in terms of step-by-step operations, and *functional components*—a statement of the mechanisms which are necessary to support the process model. For many process models concerned with thinking, judging, deciding and understanding, the main components assumed are a very large rapid-access permanent memory, and a small short-term and working memory where much of the information is processed in various ways. This picture enables thinking to be thought about in a relatively concrete way. Let us go on to consider a simple information processing description of a rather more complex thinking task than we have hitherto encountered.

A BASIC TRANSFORMATION PROBLEM

Shortly after arriving in Glasgow, I was talking to a colleague about the geography of the place. He introduced me to the joke about a foreigner from Edinburgh who once

asked directions from A to B in Glasgow, only to be told
'Oh, you can't get there from here'.

The essence of problem-solving is the discovery and utilis-
ation of the means by which you can get from here (the
problem statement) to there (the goal statement).

Consider the concrete example shown in Figure 1.1. This
is known as the Tower of Hanoi problem, and has given
children and cognitive scientists something to puzzle over for
a very long time. In this problem, there is only one kind of
means which can be used to get from here to there, and that
is the single 'operator' MOVE DISC X to POLE Y, where X
and Y are just variables. With such an easy problem, it is
obvious that the goal can be achieved. An important part of
the problem, however, is to reach the goal state in as few
moves as possible. How might this be achieved?

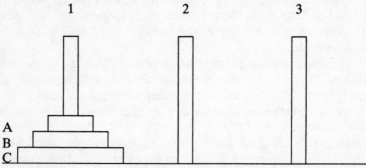

*1.1   The tower of Hanoi problem with three discs. The problem is to move
the discs from the pole they are on at the start to one of the other poles
(which is specified). A disc may not be placed on top of a smaller disc, and
only one disc at a time may be moved.*

One method, sometimes adopted by children on first exposure to the problem, is to move the discs around at random, physically enacting possible move sequences. Adults
sometimes fall back on this too when the number of discs
is increased to four or five or more. But such random behaviour usually requires considerable persistence to get the
solution pattern, and this is almost invariably at the cost of
extra moves. To see why, Figure 1.2 shows a network from
which can be derived all of the possible move sequences
within the problem. To derive a possible move sequence,

begin at the start point and select a route to an adjacent
point. Notice that there is choice even if one does not elect
to move back to a position from which one has just come,
and that it is possible for quite long move sequences to take
you back to a position where you have been before. In the
absence of this diagram, a trial-and-error method would
have to rely upon a person being able to recognise a previously encountered state, otherwise it is possible in principle to keep going for ever. With more discs the number of
possible states increases dramatically.

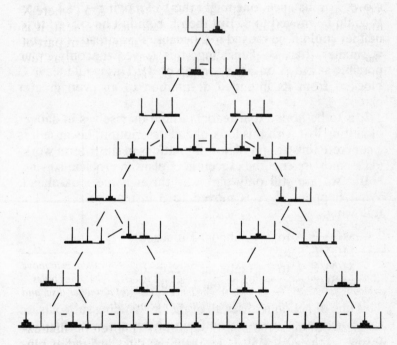

*1.2   A network of all possible transitions between problem states. The left
vertex is the start state, the top vertex is the goal state.*

Most people approach the problem in a far superior way
to that of randomly generating new states. After all, people
are intelligent, and blind search is not intelligent. People
adopt specific sorts of strategy, and these strategies and the
limits on their applicability can be most readily understood

in information processing terms. We shall consider one sort of strategy which leads to a solution.[10]

First, note that in order to succeed, disc C has to be the first to be placed on pole 3. Let us call this objective *subgoal 1*. To do this, A and B have to be moved. Call this *subgoal 2*. To do this, A must be moved first: this is *subgoal 3*. There is nothing to prevent disc A from being moved at this point. However, there is the problem of where it should be moved to. One way in which people may tackle this problem is to look ahead by imagining the consequences of any particular move. For instance, one might think of moving A to 2. Then B could be moved to 3. But then C couldn't be moved to 3; neither could B be moved to 2 because A is already on it and is smaller than B. Persisting, this leaves the only move possible as put A on 3 (i.e. on top of B). This would leave C blocked from its intended destination to an even greater extent!

It is to be hoped that readers found themselves in danger of getting lost with this look-ahead description, because it is a concrete illustration of how limitations in short-term working memory restrict the execution of plans in problem-solving.

But we are still only part way through the look-ahead. What happens if A is moved to 3 instead of to 2? The following:

MOVE A to 3   (subgoal 3 realised)
MOVE B to 2
MOVE A to 2   (subgoal 2 realised)
MOVE C to 3   (subgoal 1 realised)

This line of action realises all of the outstanding subgoals, so these actions can be carried out. Now a new subgoal is produced: MOVE B to 3. The same sort of chain of subgoals and look-ahead goes on again, but there are fewer subgoals so it is easier. To get the flavour, readers are invited at this point to work out subgoals and look-ahead for the remainder of the problem.

Problem-solving has received a great deal of attention in recent years from both computer scientists and psychologists. The Tower of Hanoi puzzle is typical of one particularly well-studied set known as transformation problems, a set which includes somewhat more practical problems such as working out proofs in symbolic logic and mathematics. The essential characteristics of transformation puzzles are a well-defined start-state, a well-defined goal-state, and a well-defined set of operators to change from one problem state to another. It is easy to see how maths proofs fall into this category; in algebra, for example, what one has is a string of symbols to start with, a string of symbols as a goal, and the problem is to select and apply the appropriate operators to transform one into the other. The series of steps constitutes the solution. The operators express the rules of algebra, which themselves are no more than allowable transitions from one string of symbols to another.

ELABORATING PROCESSES IN PROBLEM-SOLVING

Simple transition problems serve to illustrate the way in which working memory limitations cause difficulties in thinking. This is particularly obvious when the number of operators is small but the number of possible states is large, as in a many-disc Tower of Hanoi problem, or noughts and crosses. While memory limitations are in fact at issue with most types of problem, some problems serve to illustrate how the amazing flexibility of long-term memory can offset the difficulties of working memory.

Consider a simple anagram problem, for example. The following set of letters can be rearranged to make a commonplace English word:

{C, E, A, R, I, F, L, P, E}

What possible strategies are there for solving this? Well, there is no point in drawing out an arrangement of letters diagram as we did for possible arrangements of discs in the Tower of Hanoi problem. There are no fewer than 362,880 possible arrangements of nine letters! What this means is that this readily solved anagram cannot be solved by a process of exhaustively generating and testing every letter combination, for although after a very, very long time it would reveal the answer, it would not be making much use of information which all of us have in long-term memory. The information concerns how words are made up, and words which we as individuals *know* are words. This general knowledge can be used to constrain the letter sequences which are produced.

For convenience, I shall call the process of playing with initial combinations stem-generation. Stem-generation occurs when a few of the letters are selected for combination to begin with. Suppose that we begin by taking three or four letters and arranging them to see what they suggest. This still leaves a lot of possibilities open, but it is quite easy to constrain choice. A sensible method is to select letters in a combination such that the stem produced looks like part of a word. And a typical rule within this method might be to have at least one vowel and one consonant in the combination. (Stem sets typically contain more than two letters, of course.)

Another principle of the same type is to find stems which are themselves words. Either way, in our example we may find combinations like FIRE, PEAR, PEAL, LEAP, and so on. The stems will not be exhaustive, of course.

Given the idea of stem-generation, further processes become possible. Stem-generation produces parts of possible words, or words themselves, as above, and these stems can be used as the basis of a further constrained search. This further process could work in a number of ways. One way is that the stem could trigger words directly. For example, PEAR may trigger PEARDROPS. But a quick test would cause this to be rejected, since with PEAR taken out of the letter set, the residue is FCIEL, which cannot form DROP, of course. With the stem FIRE on the other hand, FIREPLACE might be triggered, and this would be fine, since the residue CALPE can form PLACE.

Obviously, most of the stems produced will not lead anywhere, and will in any case suggest unworkable completions, but even the straightforward use of lexical and orthographic knowledge mentioned above will rule out a large number of possible letter combinations which are useless, such as E, A, I, E, R, C, F, L, P, and so on.

While the reader should understand that what is offered above is only one small part of the processing possibilities for anagram solution, I am using it to illustrate an important principle: Whenever possible, pertinent knowledge which we possess (i.e. which is stored in long-term memory) will be used to aid problem solutions by constraining the space of possibilities which characterise blindly applying an operator and testing the outcome at random. This, in turn, reduces the load on working memory, and in many cases makes it *possible* to get to a solution at all.

Both parts of the method for anagram testing, stem-generation and memory triggering rely upon the remarkable way in which long-term memory is accessed. We know literally thousands of words. Yet stems suggest words to us with little difficulty, and in a seemingly automatic and un-intentional way, stems are selected using orthographic principles which are represented in some form in long-term memory. From a conscious point of view, the most difficult aspect of the problem is what to do when these complex automatic processes do not seem to be leading anywhere. The mechanisms by which information is recovered from long-term memory so automatically, and (usually) appropriately is one of the most important challenges facing us today.[11]

The fact is that all problem-solving relies upon the application of knowledge stored in long-term memory. Sometimes this knowledge is extremely simple. In the case of the Tower of Hanoi, the minimal knowledge requirement is the problem description itself, including the operator, the one move at a time rule, and the disc size constraint. With a comparable real-life problem, such as 'How can you (the reader) visit a friend in Las Cruces, New Mexico?', the machinery of setting goals and subgoals is entirely appropriate. But the operators involved come from long-term memory and are not part of the problem statement itself. Planning depends upon general knowledge about the use of taxis, aeroplanes, trains, the distances covered by these kinds of transport, the fact that trains do not cross oceans, and so on. These pieces of data are necessary both for the definition of operators and for planning in general. Of course, it is what we might call *mundane* knowledge, in the sense of being everyday, but this does not make it any the less important.

We possess a great deal of mundane knowledge which is used in problem-solving. Most people do not possess a great deal of specialist knowledge, however. For instance, take the problem: given $p \rightarrow q$, prove (i.e. get to) $-q \rightarrow -p$. This will be nonsense to most people, but to someone who knows the 'expert' domain of symbolic logic, it will bring to mind a basic operator set (the rules of logic) [12] which provide the means to construct a proof. The logician can do this because she knows the rules and their range of application, and no more. Mundane knowledge—the facts, rules and procedures depicting everyday actions—are known to almost all people in a given culture, while expert domains are known to only a few. Beyond this, there are no real differences between them from an information processing point of view.

Let me finish this brief illustration of the role of knowledge in long-term memory with an experimental study. In this investigation, American college students were presented with algebra problems in verbal rather than in symbolic form. It was found that many of the students could say what 'kind' of problem they were hearing after less than one-fifth of each one had been presented.[13] *Kind* of problem means that problems belonging to a particular *kind* could be tackled in a particular, stereotyped way. This certainly demonstrates the speed and automaticity of accessing the appropriate information in long-term memory.

SUMMARY

The idea behind this chapter was to show how, by adopting an information processing point of view, sensible things could be said about thinking and related psychological activities. The idea that we have enough facts about thought processes available to us from introspection was shown to be inadequate in a number of ways. It is difficult to assess the reliability of introspections in many cases. Indeed, sometimes it is even a problem to know what reliability means in the context of introspection.[14] Not only is it often difficult to describe the nature of our introspections, but with many tasks where mental activity has taken place, there is apparently little or nothing available to us to report.

Understanding happens when the mystery is taken away from things, and one of the more successful attempts to take the mystery out of thought itself has been to think of mental life in terms of information processing. No matter how each event and piece of information is coded (in the brain cells, presumably) it is possible to describe certain mental activities as a chain of events (the result of running a process model) which take place within functional components of the system. Although our understanding can only be enhanced by discovering how these functional components relate to brain anatomy and physiology, we do not need to know how they are before extensive use can be made of information-processing models. While reserving discussion of the implications of this point of view for a picture of human nature until later chapters, let us take a little temporary comfort in the fact that information-processing models make thinking sound rather mechanical. Viewing the body as a machine was at one time unthinkable, yet the result of thinking this way is modern medicine rather than magic (so why not the mind?). And we can understand machines because it is transparent that A causes B which causes C etc., until we see clearly how, in a machine, we get from 'here to there' (so why not look at thinking this way?).[15]

The main components which have been introduced are working memory, short-term memory and long-term memory. The limited capacity of the first two were shown to influence the likelihood of succeeding in a simple problem, the Tower of Hanoi. The implications of this are potentially enormous: Even when we are tackling a problem in a perfectly rational way, we may get the solution wrong because of a limit in working memory. This is not just a system limitation, since while all is well if we know we have failed, if we get the answer wrong but do not know that we have, then there will be a basis for having a false belief. With social problem-solving we would be right in calling this a failure of human nature.

Our other simple example was the anagram. This was used to illustrate how knowledge (data in long-term memory)

is brought to bear very easily on a problem so as to reduce
the amount of work which the problem requires, and so to
reduce potential loads on working memory. We may summarise by putting forward two well-recognised properties of
human functional components:

1. A very limited space where certain types of information
   (such as goals and plans) are saved and manipulated.
2. An enormous long-term memory from which problem-
   relevant data come forth with amazing ease and rapidity.

Armed with these rudimentary concepts, we are ready to
embark on our explorations of human understanding.

CHAPTER 2

Aspects of Understanding Language

Language plays a central role in the life of mankind. Sequences of speech sounds and squiggles on a piece of paper have led to lives being saved, wars being started, and learning things great and small. Speech enables people to learn something of things they have not themselves seen or experienced. The invention of writing systems enables people to learn of things created long ago and far away. This experience by proxy does indeed enable man to broaden his range of experience far beyond that of other creatures.

Our interest in language within the general theme of this book is not with language *per se*. Rather it depends upon the fact that language in use is closely related to the more general problem of what it is to understand anything. For not only is language understanding important in its own right, but I believe it to be a clue to a much broader range of cognitive activities. In many ways, the present chapter provides a foundation for the study of these broader issues. Furthermore, the present chapter serves to give a little insight into what is involved in trying to develop process models as outlined in the previous chapter.

Language and thought are of course intimately related. What we say is the product of thinking, however deep or however shallow, and what we take people to mean depends upon our interpretation, which is itself a thought process. Some people even believe that they think in words—certainly, on occasion, people will talk to themselves when they are thinking. However, as I shall argue, I think it is more realistic to say that not only do we *not* think in words, but we

do not understand language in words either. Words manipulate mechanisms of thought, and thought processes select
the words which we utter, but words themselves are only
sounds or shapes which interact with mental procedures.

While I shall try to convey some of the computational complexity of understanding language, one must not forget how
easy human beings find it to use, as a rule. People who are
not sufficiently intelligent to solve even very simple problems
can still hold conversations and listen to the radio, and understand quite well. That is not to say that they may not have
problems in communicating, or that they may not be limited
in what they talk about. But it is saying that the complexity
behind what they do with language—the amount of inference that goes on, as we shall see—is remarkable when one
considers their poor performance as problem-solvers. Much
of language processing is automatic, and these automatic
processes underlie more general aspects of understanding.

Language has been much studied throughout the course of
recorded history—the invention of writing systems enables
us to know that. Work on grammar is found in early Sanskrit
writings as well as in the more familiar works of the ancient
Greeks.[1] Linguistics, as an independent scientific subject in
the modern sense, emerged in the late nineteenth century.
More recently, computer scientists began to concern themselves with machine translation, a topic of considerable practical importance. The appalling difficulties which they encountered gave a great boost to the study of language from linguistic
and computational viewpoints.[2] It should be added that if we
wish a computer to act upon instructions given in natural
language, then it must mimic understanding to an appropriate
degree. As with problem-solving, psychologists have greatly
benefited from the problems and issues revealed by the
efforts of computer scientists to program aspects of human
language understanding. Indeed, language studies is one of
the cornerstones of the cognitive science movement.

PRELIMINARIES

Because of our familiarity with the characters that make up
our language, it is all too easy to underestimate that which

must be involved in a full account of language processing. A page of Urdu, or modern Korean, or some other language with which one is unfamiliar will bring the point home.[3] Any processing account of written language understanding must begin with character recognition, the very perceptual act of recognising meaningful units from what are literally lines and squiggles on a page. From that point upwards one could add interpreting how the units are put together into sentences, interpreting the relations between each of the sentences, somehow integrating all of the information to understand the significance of the message as a whole.

We shall certainly not be concerned with the whole process, and we shall not be concerned with any language except English; the illustration is merely a reminder of what the global problem is whenever we think about natural language understanding. For our purposes, it is not necessary to describe research work on pattern and word recognition, or even on syntax, although these are essential and well-studied aspects of language processing.[4] We shall only introduce them when they play an obvious role in higher-level aspects of understanding.

To begin, it is necessary to decide what it might mean to say that understanding has taken place. Here are some possible things that someone who has understood a discourse might do with it:

1. *Summarise it.* If a discourse is of any length, the production of a summary could be said to indicate understanding. Summaries are usually shorter in length than originals, and can be said to capture the 'gist' or the 'point' of the discourse. For instance, a summary of what has been said up to now in this chapter might look like this:
   'The writer has introduced language understanding as an important part of understanding in general. Discussing how it is understood in information processing terms will also illustrate more of what is meant by a process model', etc.
   To produce a summary requires understanding.
2. *Paraphrase it.* Paraphrases are closely related to summaries, and require the wording to be changed while preserving the original meaning. This in turn requires the separation of meaning from wording, of course.

3. *Answer questions based on inference from the discourse.*
This can go on at any level. And theoretically there is no
limit to the number of inferences which could be drawn
from a discourse. But inferences differ in relevance and
plausibility, and so will be restricted in practice. What is
clear is that many inferences *are* made by human under-
standers. Consider the following:

John wanted to see his aunt in Australia.
He travelled by 'plane.

An important inference made by just about everyone in
the face of this example is revealed by responses to the
question: Did John go by 'plane to see his aunt? Although
the usual answer is 'yes', this answer cannot be directly
deduced from the content of the two-line discourse. In
fact, there is no *explicit* connection between the two,
except that John is the subject of both sentences. Rather,
it is our understanding that links them through inference.
Perhaps the chain is something like: John wants to see his
aunt, so presumably this is his main goal (as far as the
narrative is concerned), so when he does something which
is plausible as an action in the service of that goal, then it
is indeed to be taken as being in the service of that goal.
Going on a 'plane fits the bill.

Although straightforward, if understanding takes place,
we can expect to find many inferences similar to this to
have been made.

4. *Act and think in response to the message.* In the case of
simple spoken messages, simple overt actions are often
called for:

'Open the door.'
'Would you open the door, please?'

In a compliant state of mind, an understanding of the
first example would result in the door being opened. It is
a simple command. In the second case, the request is
actually couched as a question. Unless tongue in cheek, a
response of 'yes' would indicate a lack of understanding
(more inference here, of course).

Bill: 'Have you got the screwdriver?'
Ben: 'It's in the toolbox.'

Ben doesn't say 'no' (though he could choose to do so).

Rather, he infers that Bill wants the screwdriver. So he cooperates and tells him where it is. These examples show how actions, and the thoughts which underlie them, demonstrate comprehension.[5]

Indeed, it is one of the key features of discourse that it seems to be based on an implicit contract.[6] Essentially, each participant in a dialogue must do several things. In particular, they must try to present information in a way which fits in some manner with each other's expectations, and which is essentially unambiguous. The mechanisms by which this is achieved are a topic of much enquiry, for while it is easy to see when a failure occurs, it is difficult to characterise the conditions which must hold to meet the goal.

A SAMPLE OF DISCOURSE PROCESSING ISSUES

Our list of criteria for understanding, although sketchy and incomplete, serves to show at least some of the things which have to be considered when trying to work out a process model. Now we have to look at a few features of understanding in more detail. Because most of these implicate mechanisms which one would normally consider to be automatic and unconscious, we shall refer to the machinery which does the work as 'the processor'. It sounds less strange than saying that the 'reader' does these things, even if they do actually happen in the reader's brain. In any case, if an explanation can be formulated as a process model, an ingenious programmer should be able to construct a computer program which carries out the same operations.

To begin, let us notice that in order to meet criterion (3) above—answer questions based on inference—it is clearly necessary that a processor builds some sort of representation which goes beyond the words of the text. One way in which this can be demonstrated is through the phenomenon of *situational anaphora*. (Anaphora is a term used to describe a case where a previously introduced term is referred to again using a different expression.) The simplest case is perhaps the use of a pronoun, as in:

John was on his way to school.

He was worried about the maths lesson.

In the first sentence, a character is introduced through the expression *John*. In the second line, the expression *John* is not used to refer to the character, but instead the anaphor *He* is used. It is clear to a human reader that *John* and *He* designate the same individual, but even this requires some work on the part of the processor. For instance, one possibility is that when the processor encounters the term *John*, it retrieves from the long-term memory knowledge-base the fact that John must be male, human (probably), and is a particular (singular) character. Later, on encountering the pronoun *He*, the processor may look up the fact that 'He' is a term used for a male, probably human, singular entity, again from the long-term database. Then, on the basis of having found a pronoun, a search might be set up between the pattern of information retrieved when the pronoun was encountered and some matching representation which has resulted from the prior discourse. Such a representation is 'attached' to the label *John*. So the processor has established that *John* and *He* designate the same individual.

This may sound long-winded, but the principle is simple. When a pronoun is encountered, a search of a representation of the prior text must take place if the pronoun is to be matched to anything at all. And of course, if a pronoun is encountered for which there is no match, the result is unintelligibility at a very basic level. Lewis Carroll made use of this fact in the following snippet from Alice in Wonderland:

> I gave her one, they gave him two,
> You gave us three or more:
> They all returned from him to you,
> Though they were mine before.

Details of processing accounts of pronoun usage have received considerable attention recently, and some headway into solving some of the complexities has been made.[7] In essence, the account sketched out above is not too misleading. But let us turn to a different kind of anaphora, that which is called an epithet:

A 'plane came plummeting from the sky.
A boy pointed excitedly at the stricken 747.
This time we all recognise that *'plane* and *stricken 747* designate the same entity. How? Well, the problem is similar to that of the pronoun. At some point the processor must establish that *stricken 747* = *'plane* by retrieving data from long-term memory that says something like 'A 747 IS A KIND OF 'PLANE', and recognising both phrases as singular, it draws the appropriate deduction. Once again, this implies some sort of search process.

These are straightforward cases of anaphora, but nevertheless they serve to show how general knowledge is necessary to achieve any kind of coherence in understanding a text. But the most interesting case for the present purpose is *situational* anaphora, as promised. Consider the following examples:

(1) Max drove to Dover. The car ran well.

(2) Max went to the pub. The barmaid was charming.

In (1), we read *The car* . . . . How did a car get into it? No car was mentioned in the preceding sentence. Yet to understand the message is to understand that the car is the one that Max used when he drove to Dover. A processor must be able to take a noun phrase when one is encountered and search a prior representation of the discourse to find an entity which is implied by a statement of action. In the case of (1), driving implies using a car, so presumably this piece of data is retrieved from long-term memory, and used to establish that in the message, *'the car'* is the car that Max is driving to Dover. Although it may be argued that driving entails using a car, it is still necessary to specify the means by which such a fact could be used by the processor.

The second example illustrates a similar point. Introducing *the barmaid* makes immediate sense, but requires the processor to recognise that 'barmaid' is what it would expect to find at a pub. This is true situational anaphora, since the verb 'to go' cannot possibly be the source of such information. Rather, it is our understanding of the whole event depicted by the first sentence of (2) which gives the processor access to the situation—Max is at the pub—and it is general knowledge about what is found in pubs which enables the processor to appreciate in some way that this is the barmaid at the pub which Max is in. Hence the convenient label of situational anaphora.

Situational and other anaphoric processes are obviously central to discourse understanding. If we (or a processor) do not recognise how the various referring expressions of a text fit together, then in no way can the message be said to be understood. Yet it is necessary to go far beyond the words on the page to meet this criterion of referential cohesion. In fact, short of automatically carrying out processes like those outlined above, there is really nothing to connect the two sentence-pairs above given in the words themselves.

I am leading up to the argument that the mental representation of a piece of discourse is not a mere record of the words themselves, but is a record of the interpretation of the message. And this interpretation has to occur fairly early on if the processor is to make sense of later parts of the message.[8] The idea is that early interpretation can guide a processor in making later interpretations. This raises the question of how it all gets started, of course, and this will be discussed shortly. But first I wish to illustrate some other phenomena which have a direct bearing on the argument. These can best be introduced with the following example:

> John was on his way to school last Friday.
> He was really worried about the maths lesson.

A simple enough situation, one might suppose. Now read the next sentence:

> Last week he was unable to control the class.

If you are like most readers, you will find this sentence slightly strange. In all probability, you unwittingly assumed that John was a schoolboy, and to fit in the third sentence, you had to change your view. People seem to make these assumptions automatically, and it is only when some tricky writer capitalises on the fact in a rather unkind fashion that this leads to trouble:

> John was on his way to school last Friday. He was really worried about the maths lesson. Last week he had been unable to control the class. It was unfair of the maths teacher to keep leaving him in charge. After all, it is not a normal part of the janitor's duties.

Seemingly, in order to make sense of this passage, we need to make assumptions about the role that John occupies. This seems to be an automatic process which can be revealed by breaking the assumptions. Of course, any writer who does this knows that he is breaking his 'contract' with the reader, and will only do it to achieve some special rhetorical effect.

One general method for revealing how far people go beyond the words of a discourse is to produce examples which perhaps violate the assumptions an investigator is trying to get at. For instance, the following reveals an interesting property:

The secretary picked up the dictation pad.

He hated taking shorthand.

In this case things are just a little strange because in our present culture secretaries are almost always female, and *he* is a masculine pronoun. Quite obviously, in order to match the pronoun to the antecedent noun, a test has to be made for a 'singular, male, human', and the data associated with secretary do not quite fit the bill in the first instance.

Fortunately, the consequences of assumptions such as these can be measured in a relatively simple way. Subjects can be asked to look at a screen, and press a button to get the 'next sentence' of a piece of discourse. After a little practice, subjects happily press away, reading their way through whatever material the experimenter wishes. At the same time, it is easy for the computer controlling the display to measure how long people dwell on any given sentence before calling up the next one. Although these dwell times are usually very short, fortunately they are also sensitive to the phenomena described above, as well as to others. For instance, in the example directly above, the second sentence takes longer to read when the pronoun is 'he' than if it were 'she'. One can conclude that the processor has indeed encountered a gender mismatch which has caused it a problem that took time to solve.[9]

By the same technique, it has been shown that with examples like 'John the schoolboy' the sentence 'Last week he was unable to control the class' takes longer to read when the term *John* is used than when the expression *The schoolmaster* is substituted. One can thus conclude that the assumptions which I am claiming are made, appear to be made in fact, and that these are reflected in the reading time differences.[10]

One final example: reading time analyses reveal something interesting about situational anaphora. If subjects are reading a story about, say, being in court, a sentence like 'The lawyer was trying to prove his innocence' is read more quickly than is the same sentence in a more general, but compatible, context headed 'telling a lie'. This vindicates the view that expressions which fit an expectancy pattern based on the prior discourse are accommodated into the processor's representation more easily than are expressions which have to be made to fit when they are encountered.[11]

This somewhat detailed excursion into the conceptual and experimental study of discourse processes puts at least some meat on the bones of our basic argument. Text (and speech)[12] consists of words ordered within the constraints of syntax. These words serve to trigger off mental processes, which generate inferences, presuppositions and expectations. All of these not only guide future interpretations as one carries on reading or listening, but they are ultimately the 'understood' message itself. Before going on to describe how a processing system might work, let us leave the present discussion of going beyond the written word with a puzzle which some readers may not have encountered:

> A man and his son were away for a trip. They were driving along the motorway when they had a terrible accident. The man was killed outright, but his son was alive though badly injured. The boy was rushed to hospital for emergency surgery. On entering the operating theatre, the surgeon said in a shocked state: 'I can't do this operation. This boy is my son.'

How can this be explained?

PRIMARY PROCESSING SOLVES PROBLEMS

It is quite clear that a major aspect of understanding is the interpretation of what is to be understood in terms of what one already knows. It is also apparent that such interpretation may serve to solve some of the problems discussed above—problems which concern the very means by which discourse is processed. The idea that interpretation is the act of relating an input to what is already known may sound fairly trivial, but it is not. In a nutshell, the argument clearly requires the following assumptions to be met within any processing system which could sustain it:

(a) There are knowledge (data) structures in long-term memory to which a message may be related, and

(b) There are procedures by which messages are brought into useful relationships with the knowledge structures.

At once, this raises a host of questions. What kind of 'knowledge structures' do humans possess? Given that the knowledge each one of us must possess is going to be quite astronomical in quantity, how does the *appropriate* knowledge come to be selected? How many of the problems of producing an integrated, coherent view of a message can actually be accommodated by looking at things in this way, and what are the major problems? Much practical and theoretical research has gone into exploring and debating these questions in recent years, and so some headway can be made towards answering them.

First, the matter of the kinds of knowledge structures which one might expect to find in human long-term memory. This issue has two aspects: *content* and *form*. By content is meant knowledge of 'what', and by form is meant how that knowledge is organised. It is easier to understand the first. Quite obviously, we possess a vast amount of knowledge, most of it to do with quite normal everyday things, some of it to do with our own individual expertise and interests. Some of the knowledge we possess is accessible to us in that we can describe it, and some of it is not accessible. An example of the former might be 'how to make an omelette', while an example of the latter is 'how to ride a bicycle'.[13] It is the former class of knowledge which is most obviously related to language understanding, rather than the latter class of 'skills'.

One type of knowledge which I wish to emphasise is *stereotypical* knowledge. We all have stereotypical knowledge of what a university professor is supposed to be like,— that he will read a lot, that he will probably be male, etc. We have stereotypical knowledge of what to expect to see at a football match, of what the normal course of events will be when we pay a visit to the cinema, or go to a restaurant for a meal. Stereotypical knowledge can embody expectations about people, situations, and likely courses of action. Furthermore, as the term 'stereotypical' implies, anyone of us confidently expects his neighbour to have the same knowledge. Now it has been argued extensively that such knowledge is precisely the kind of thing which people learn, indeed have to learn, simply as a function of being in society.[14] Social chaos would reign if we all had radically different expectations of all situations, or could rely upon no one to conform to the conventions of various situations. Similarly, in order to produce an omelette, boil an egg, replace a light-bulb, and so on for other constrained activities, the procedures employed and the things used are quite stereotyped, although in these instances it can be the physical rather than social constraints which bring about the rigidity.

These kinds of stereotypes have been considered as possible candidates for the basis of understanding by a number of workers. Perhaps the best-known schemes of this sort are due to Schank and Abelson,[15] who use the term 'script' as a label for a package of knowledge which contains stereotypical information, and Minsky,[16] who uses the term 'frame' for similar data structures. In essence, the idea is that long-term memory contains modules of information which are like recipes for situational and other stereotypes, and that these are used, where possible, as a basis for understanding.

This idea is sufficiently central to our purpose to warrant illustration. Suppose that one's knowledge of what happens at a cinema is something like the 'script' shown below:

> *Cinema expectations from patron's view*
> Requirements: Patron wishes to see film
>   Patron has money
> Cast: Patron, cashier, usherette
> Action sequence:

1. Customer enters cinema
2. Customer buys ticket from cashier
3. Customer goes to auditorium door
4. Customer gives ticket to usherette
5. Usherette gives half ticket to customer
6. Usherette leads customer to seat
7. Customer sits down
8. CUSTOMER WATCHES FILM TO END
9. Customer leaves

A script gets its name from being like a theatre script. Notice that the level of detail given in this is not particularly great, and that each of the action lines are themselves capable of further description. They are not specified because these actions are more general than cinema-specific acts. For instance, sitting down could be described as a series of actions—movements, orientations of the body, etc.—and is undertaken with the goal of being in a certain position at the end. Sitting down has requirements like there is something to sit on, etc. It too is a possible candidate for a 'sitting-down script', but is applicable to a wide range of circumstances, and can be taken for granted in the cinema script.

Now back to discourse, in the form of an example:

Max went to the cinema to see the latest Western.

The usherette showed him to a very good seat.

Let us suppose that on encountering the first sentence, the processor establishes that Max, a person, is *at a cinema*—the result of executing the process of 'going to somewhere'. He wants to see a Western, which the processor discovers from long-term memory is a kind of film. A goal to see a film and being at a cinema should be enough to activate (make available for use) the cinema script. Once the script is available, the first sentence can be interpreted into the script. A check for a character in the script to match *John* to finds <CUSTOMER>, where the notation indicates that 'customer' is a script datastructure. Similarly, *Western* finds <FILM>. (We shall not discuss the processing details of this.[17]) We can now say that Max and Western are mapped into customer and film 'slots' in the script. Now consider the second sentence. The first phrase is *The usherette*. This finds <USHERETTE> in the script. Effectively, this mapping makes it clear that the usherette is *the usherette at the cinema that John is at,* one of those assumptions which humans make so easily, which is so vital, and which is all too easy to overlook. The rest of the sentence matches the action description number 6, and provides a little extra: the seat is a good one.

This all seems very straightforward, and does buy us quite a lot in the way of understanding. For instance, on being asked whether Max had bought a ticket, the system would be able to infer something like 'I expect so', since action 6 stereotypically depends upon the completion of action 3. In a similar way, if a text input does *not* fit the action stereotype properly, then the script still provides a foundation for understanding:

Max went into the cinema to see a film.

The cashier refused to give him a ticket.

Basically, all there is to understand here is that something abnormal has happened. Because the first line cues the script, and the second introduces *cashier* and *ticket*, action 2 is identifiable as the action in question. However, the details of the action depicted do not match the details of the script-action, so effectively an abnormal condition is recognised. In such cases, what is required is some sort of explanation, and normally a writer would provide one in the near future, if the principles of cooperation are met:

Max went into the cinema to see a film. The cashier refused to give him a ticket. She said that he was drunk.

A key feature of the script notion is that it provides what is termed *default* information; that is, a statement of what normally to expect in a situation. The same idea is key in Minsky's[18] more generalised notion of a frame. Minsky discusses the idea of a 'room' frame for instance. How would you define a room? Well, it's in a building, has walls (usually four), has a ceiling, etc. Note how there is the default 'usually four'. One could add that these are usually at right-angles to one another, the floor area has to be in excess of a certain value (normally more than 1.5 square metres), that the length to breadth ratio has to be within certain bounds, etc. After all, what would you think if you were offered an office 12 metres × 1.5 metres? 'More like a corridor', no doubt. Or 1.5 × 1.5 metres?—'More like a cupboard'.

This inadequate set of specifications for a room gives some insight into aspects of Minsky's idea. First, socially meaningful situations, objects in the world, action sequences, and a variety of other things, can be described as sets of expectations (some perhaps necessary, some merely typical).[19] Scripts are thus a subset of frames, which contain 'what to do' information. There would be no actions in a room frame, for instance. Frames are presumed to be brought into play to enable fundamental understanding. For instance, to know that you are in a room, it is presumed that the features of the room match the room-frame datastructure. If the room is circular, you should notice that fact because it mismatches the default on wall number and geometry. If it is the wrong shape altogether—too small for instance—you should notice this too. Obviously, given a room frame it is possible to refer to anything in it and make sense, so it enables situational anaphora. In Minsky's view, special procedures can also be part of the frame's datastructure. For instance, if the room is too small, then a procedure in the frame might indicate that it is a cupboard. If it has too many doors and is the wrong geometry, call it a corridor, and so on. This amounts to a claim that frames are built into frame systems, where related but different sorts of things are explicitly related but different. This has a number of advantages, including allowing one to understand things like 'He called it a room, but to Mary it was more like a cupboard'. Another advantage is that it fits the way in which many things are learned. Thus, to a small infant, an attribute framework for an adult male may have 'call this Dada' attached to it at one stage, followed a little later by 'IF–NOT a particular man, call it *man*'.

We have strayed somewhat from language, but we are not meandering. Frame-type datastructures can enable a very simple but truly fundamental type of understanding. My claim is that understanding is founded on what I shall term *primary processing*: for any given input, find a datastructure to which it bears the strongest relation, and interpret new things in terms of this until a new datastructure has to be used.

It is of course difficult to investigate the structure of human memory in these terms, and so to answer a question such as 'Is human memory made up, in the main or at all, of frame-like structures?' requires rather indirect methods. One of the burdens of the chapters which follow is to show that primary processing, which relies upon something like frames, explains not only aspects of understanding, but also errors of judgement.

For the time being, let us simply note that humans do possess situation-specific stereotyped knowledge, and that such knowledge is indeed essential. In fact, let us go further and note that any particular *individual* may have frame-like structures about things which are unique to *him*. For instance, someone who worked in a garage would have more situation-specific knowledge for testing a faulty car engine, than the average driver who fills his car with petrol whenever it breaks down.

PSYCHOLOGICAL ASPECTS OF PRIMARY PROCESSING

A fully-fledged process model of text understanding based on the lines discussed above requires considerable extra machinery to be workable, but the viability of the account is illustrated by the fact that script-based and frame-based understanding systems have been implemented in working computer programs. This, of course, does not mean that *human* understanding works in exactly the same way, only that it is possible to make a system work which is based on these principles. To talk of process models of this type is at least more than wishful thinking.

For our purposes, it is appropriate to examine the claim that situation-specific knowledge is imported into the understanding process as understanding proceeds, and that the result of this importation is that default information is somehow treated as 'given' by the text that is being understood. In fact, such evidence comes from a number of different sources.

The first and most obvious source is the experimental work on situational anaphora, discussed earlier. If a piece of language input suggests a more complete 'scene' (as a fragment might suggest a script in script theory), then one would expect entities which are defaults in that scene to be available to the processor. Thus, a statement to the effect that 'John is in court' enables the processor quickly to resolve a reference to 'the lawyer', because 'lawyer' is a default of that scene. In contrast, if we are only told that 'John is telling a lie', a mention of 'the lawyer' will take longer to process, because although it can perhaps be fitted in, it is not 'given' in the current background knowledge scene. This processing time difference was exactly what appeared in the self-paced reading situation introduced on p. 25.

A slightly more complex reading-time study allows for a more interesting set of conclusions.[20] Consider the following text:

At the Cinema
Jenny found the film boring.
The projectionist had to keep changing reels.
It was supposed to be a silent classic.
Seven hours/Ten minutes later, the film was forgotten.

There are two characters in this passage, *Jenny* and *The projectionist*. Now it can be argued that Jenny will probably be thought of as a patron, by default, in a cinema setting. As such, we should not be at all surprised to find that as the story went on, Jenny left the cinema, went home, or for a meal, or whatever. The projectionist is entirely different. First, from a narrative point of view, *the projectionist* is only important within the cinema scene. Now, the final sentence in our example allows two variants. The argument is that *Seven hours later* would be checked against default knowledge of how long a cinema scene would normally last (primary process checking). As it happens, seven hours is well beyond the norm, so after encountering this version of the sentence, the processor should have registered 'cinema scene over'. This contrasts with the 'Ten minutes later . . .' version, where there would be no such outcome. Now we can combine the characters with the scene shifts. If the scene is not altered (ten minutes), we would expect to be able to refer to Jenny or the projectionist with equal ease. If the scene has been signalled as over (seven hours), we would expect to be able to refer to Jenny quite easily, since she is 'independent' of the scene. In contrast, it should be more difficult for a processor to handle a reference to the projectionist, since he is 'attached' to the cinema scene.

The results of a variety of experiments confirm this quite elaborate pattern of predictions. After a scene shift, sentences which contain references to characters attached to scenes take longer to read than they do if there is no scene shift. In contrast, sentences containing references to main characters—like Jenny—take the same amount of time to read under both circumstances.[21] Such observations are consistent with the following:

(a) When a scene is suggested by a text, a memory representation corresponding to it in full is identified in memory (primary processing).

(b) Subsequent text is matched against this representation. If a sufficient mismatch against default representation occurs (e.g. too much narrative time passes), then the background 'scene' information is no longer used to interpret.

(c) If this happens, then entities which have a major dependence on the 'scene' information will no longer be immediately available for future use, for instance as entities which can be referred to.

Essentially, such results support and refine the idea of primary processing. The processor tries to find situational knowledge in memory which matches and extends the discourse which it is processing. If this happens, then it means that the mental representation of a discourse goes far beyond the words themselves. This leads to a second group of observations about primary processing, and that is that the information pulled out of memory may be positively unhelpful in some circumstances. The puzzle posed on p. 26 illustrates this. The difficulty which many people have results from the automatic interpretation of 'surgeon' as male! The answer to the puzzle is that the surgeon is the *mother* of the injured boy. The trick text about the John–schoolboy–teacher–janitor character can be construed in the same way, as can many other so-called presupposition puzzles.[22]

There is little doubt that primary processing, the goal of

message-to-knowledge mapping, can be investigated and demonstrated. The most serious scientific questions are really those of the conditions under which a match is made. How much information is needed to make a match? What kind of information? What kind of memory structures are mapped? And so on. Closely related is the question of how quickly all of this happens. The answer to these questions goes well beyond the scope of the present book, but a few comments are in order. It appears to be a general property of the human processor that memory mapping takes place as soon as possible at as high a level as possible. The speed of relatively low-level mapping can be seen in the slight difficulty in understanding the following sentence:

The steel ships are carrying is heavy.

Did you experience anything strange when you got to 'is heavy'? If so, your processor assembled 'steel ships' as a single noun-phrase, because 'steel is a material out of which ships can be made'. If you find this fast memory-check process hard to accept, then note that people have a lot less trouble with:

The granite ships are carrying is heavy.

Such examples show the impact of early, relatively low-level primary processing.[23] Rather complex experiments are needed to show early impact of higher-level knowledge, such as scriptal or stereotyped situational information, but such experiments have been carried out.[24] At present, the primary-processing principle of early mapping seems to be supported.

IN CONCLUSION

The study of language understanding shows the extent to which knowledge of the world—mundane knowledge—is a prerequisite of understanding. A more detailed look at various processing problems reinforces this view, and indicates an intricate pattern of interactions between knowledge and process, intricate to such a degree that it is a hot topic for study in both psychology and in artificial intelligence. Illustrative problems were described to give the reader some impression of the scale of the problem.

A major concept which was introduced was termed *primary processing*. Many situations which people write about or talk about require recognition of the appropriate setting, otherwise there will be no way of beginning to comprehend the significance of many messages. It is suggested that a primary goal of the language-processing system is to connect the actual words of the utterance with data in memory which fill out the details of the setting. The primary process is thus one of finding such data and mapping the utterance onto them. This is done to the deepest necessary level as early as possible. This is perhaps a stronger claim than it sounds, since it means that the processor commits itself to a particular interpretation *at the expense of other radical alternatives* as soon as possible. Sometimes this backfires, as in the case of the character John–schoolboy–teacher–janitor. Usually it should not fail. Why? Because writers are on occasion readers and take care to try to guide readers into the appropriate mappings. When they don't, their writing is bad or difficult, or they are doing it as a special trick. The same thing happens with speakers. In conversation, speakers generally provide a setting for their utterances. But if they don't, the cost is less, since the listener can always say he doesn't understand.

Our claim is, then, that without discourse–situation matching, understanding fails at many levels. If it fails, further information will be required. Seeking this further information we shall term secondary processing, to signify that it comes about when primary processing breaks down in some way.

Finally, the outcome of the mapping process is a mental representation which goes far beyond the words of the message. This is good, because it enables understanding, but as we have seen, and shall see *par excellence*, it can bring about rather severe cases of misunderstanding and misjudgement. Primary processing is the double-edged weapon of human mentality.

CHAPTER 3

Some Tools of Thought

In this chapter we go on from the apparently simple case of discourse-to-memory mapping into the interpretation of problems and the understanding of new things. We begin with the importance of primary processing in problem understanding, and then go on to analogy-based reasoning and the idea of a mental model.

UNDERSTANDING PROBLEMS

There is a considerable difference between the interpretation of discourse and the activity of solving problems. And yet in understanding a problem, there is a similarity in that the problem statement has to be interpreted, and this will be done in relation to what is already in long-term memory. Even the very simple mathematics problems described in Chapter 1 make this clear. Given a problem like $3 + 4 = ?$, it is necessary to map the problem onto the corresponding pieces of data in memory to obtain the answer. As adults, this amounts to little more than a simple pattern match in which the answer is part of the complete pattern. A problem like $59 + 98 = ?$ is somewhat different. Unless one is a 'memory man', it is unlikely that this will be stored as a complete unit. Rather, the memory structure called up and into which the problem is mapped, consists of the set of procedures used for general purpose addition, including column rules, carry rules, etc. Yet as one sets out to apply these rules, one has already mapped the problem onto an appropriate knowledge structure. With slightly more complex problems, the structures into which mapping takes place may be more specialised. Recall that in Chapter 1 we noted a study in which students were told an algebra problem in words a little at a time. Some of the students were able to say what 'sort of problem' it was after exposure to only about a fifth of the content. What this means is that the processor made a match between the problem fragment and the long-term memory representation of a type of problem. Once a problem-type is identified, it is possible to go on to solve it.[1]

In another interesting study, Silver[2] presented three problems to seventh-grade schoolchildren. From a narrative point of view, two of the problems were very similar, referring to the same objects in a common setting (hens and rabbits in a farm). These problems required quite distinct mathematical methods for their solution, however. In contrast, one of the 'farm' problems and the remaining problem (about a collection of coins) required the application of the same mathematical principles, but differed in the objects referred to in the narrative. Silver had his young subjects decide which problem-pair was the most similar. Those children who were able to perform well at mathematical problems thought that the problems which required the same mathematical procedures were the most similar, while the others thought that the similar narrative problems were the most similar. The implication is that an appropriate mapping onto a memory structure increases in likelihood with learning, and that an ability to do well on a problem depends on making an appropriate mapping in the first place.

This may not seem particularly surprising, but it is of the greatest significance. A problem is understood in terms of what it maps onto, and perforce this limits other forms of understanding. One of my favourite examples to illustrate this is quite painful to think about. It is called the 'three cups problem'. It is easier to understand if you simulate the problem using three real cups.[3]

Imagine that you have three cups in front of you, turned upside down, as depicted in Figure 3.1a. You close your eyes for a moment and I slip a coin under one of them, but of course you do not know which (Figure 3.1b). Now I invite you to guess which cup the coin is under. You do so (Figure 3.1c). Now rather than tell you whether you are right or wrong, I remove one of the cups. As I tell you, I *never* remove the cup to which you pointed, and I *never* remove the cup that the coin is under, if it is different. These facts are made clear to you as a cup is removed (Figure 3.1d).

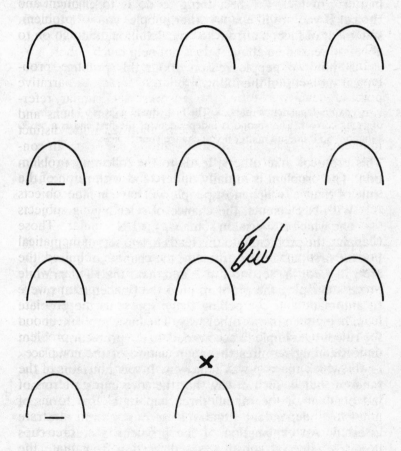

3.1   (a) *Three cups are placed upturned in front of you. You look away and* (b) *the experimenter puts a coin under one of the cups.* (c) *You guess which cup it was that the coin was placed under. Finally,* (d) *the experimenter removes one of the cups—not the one you chose, and (if different) not the one that the coin was placed under.*

You are now confronted with two cups, one which you pointed to in the first place and another one. Now I ask you to choose again. Would you rather change your choice, stick to your first choice, or doesn't it make any difference? Think about it. Almost everyone when confronted with this puzzle says that it doesn't matter so they may as well stick. Even if they change their choice, they still maintain that it doesn't matter.[4] In fact, the best thing to do is to change your choice! If you are like most other people, you will find this statement of fact an affront to your intuition, and will probably find reasoning about it does not help much either.

Just how *do* people reason about this problem? One typical subject said the following:

... two independent situations. The first situation gives a 1 in 3 chance of being correct. The second is independent of the first and is a 50–50 situation. So it doesn't matter if you change your choice.

This protocol, like others, leads to the following explanation. The problem is initially understood with respect to a 'rule of chance' which most people will have in memory:
    With N elements, the chance of selecting a particular one which is special in some way is 1/N.
Mapping the problem into this leads to two sets of mappings. For the first part of the problem, the chances of being right are 1 in 3, for the second 1 in 2, and that's that! The primary process mapping the problem onto the (inadequate) rule is so automatic and compelling that it prevents the problem from being seen in any other way. The basic problem is that the rule is too simple to accommodate the problem. A fuller understanding requires the appreciation of the conditions under which the cup was removed. It was not removed at random, but in such a way that the 'two cup state' is not independent of the initial 'three cup state', so there are not two 'independent situations' as our informant above asserted. An explanation of the problem is presented in note five, since it constitutes a digression from our main business here.

It is fairly easy to appreciate that new inputs are interpreted in terms of old memory structures, but this has little to say about the novelty of understanding, and the capacity to use knowledge which is strictly unrelated to new things to assist understanding. It is to this important topic that we now turn.

LANGUAGE CLUES TO NON-LITERAL MAPPING

The examples considered up to now give a clue as to how mapping between long-term memory structures and language input can both enable understanding to begin and also create problems of presupposition. However, we have restricted ourselves to situations where it is plausible to assume that a rather direct mapping may be made, since only literal mappings have been considered. It would scarcely do justice to the richness of language to leave matters here. Language is rich in devices above and beyond those which convey 'literal meaning'; we regularly use expressions expressing similarities between things which are quite different in a literal sense. Devices such as the simile, metaphor and analogy are rife in our everyday language as well as in the relatively rarefied world of written literature. While linguists have been interested in such things for a very long time, work in psychology on these matters has blossomed relatively recently, and in computational studies of language is still very poorly represented.[6] Yet there is little doubt that such devices reflect something rather fundamental about the way in which people think, and hence understand the world about them. Indeed, as I shall attempt to illustrate, the manifestation of these devices in language is almost certainly just the tip of an iceberg. Beneath lie some important principles of human understanding.

SIMILES, ANALOGIES AND METAPHORS

Similes have as their linguistic expression two descriptions which are usually related by what is known as the *copula of similitude*, X is like Y, and sometimes by other related expressions. They are commonplace: 'Fred is like a bull in a china shop', 'John's behaviour is like that of an idiot', 'this fog is like pea soup'. They clearly and explicitly assert a similarity between X and Y. That statements in which similarity is being asserted are not reversible may be revealed in a number of ways. One thing to note is that caveats may be explicitly stated, as in the following case: 'A zebra is like a horse, but it has stripes'.[7] Another illustration is that the relation 'is like' is not symmetric. To assert that X is like Y is very different from asserting that Y is like X, as the following example from George Miller[8] indicates:

John's wife is like his mother.
John's mother is like his wife.

As Miller points out, the first might be uttered if someone knew what John's mother is like, while the latter would be uttered if someone knew what his wife was like, but not what his mother was like. This fits a general principle in sentence structuring that the second part of a sentence serves to add information to what is known about things mentioned in the first part. Thus the first example effectively answers the question 'what new thing are you saying about John's wife?', while the second is effectively answering the question 'what new thing are you saying about John's mother?'.[9] This asymmetric feature is important from the point of view of primary processing, since it amounts to saying that when the expression is encountered the processor will attempt to map 'Mary' into some knowledge-structure about 'John's mother', in the first example. It is possible to think about similes in terms of primary processing if it is assumed that on encountering the expression 'is like', the processor will treat this as an instruction to make a mapping between X and a memory structure associated with Y. This does not solve all of the problems by any means, since it will only be selected aspects of the properties of X which will be related to selected aspects of Y.

Analogy is another term used for describing a situation where one thing is being described as being like something else. The simplest examples can be expressed within the following framework: A is to B as X is to Y. For instance, one might say 'Intuitive judgements are to linguistics as experiments are to psychology', meaning that while psychologists treat the data of experiments as that which gives

validity to their ideas, linguists treat people's judgements of
what is grammatical to give validity to their ideas. The most
notable feature of analogies looked at in this way is that they
focus on *relationships* between things. It is the relation between experiments and psychologists that is being provided
as a means of describing the relation between intuitive
judgements (of sentences) and linguists. The same argument
holds for other analogies of this sort, such as 'A woman
without a man is like a fish without a bicycle' (asserting
relationship in parallel is 'has no use for'), and 'Tirane is to
Albania as Moscow is to Russia (asserting 'is capital of').

Quite obviously, in order to appreciate these analogies, it
is necessary for a processor to access the appropriate world
knowledge. If an assertion which is made is relatively novel,
as in 'A woman without a man . . .', one can view the task
facing the processor as being one of recovering the relationship which is being implicitly asserted. This is done by establishing the 'given' relationship: there is no conceivable use a
fish could have for a bicycle, and appreciating its possible
applicability to the woman–man relationship in the mind of
someone who finds it necessary to make such an assertion.
In other cases, it may be taken for granted that the relationship will be clear, and that it needs to be applied to a pair
of things one of which is perhaps completely unknown.
Imagine a child who has not heard of Tirane, but has heard
of Albania, and who knows that Moscow is the capital of
Russia. The relationship could easily be transferred by saying 'Tirane is to Albania as Moscow is to Russia'.

The ability to learn from such analogies, and the capacity
to appreciate more remote allusions associated with them,
depends critically upon the ease with which a processor can
access the relationship which is intended. Sometimes this
may be possible because during memory search, the intended relationship comes readily to mind. For instance, 'is
capital of' is likely to be the most accessible information
relating Moscow to Russia. Thus the efficacy of an analogy
based on this relies upon the producer's sensitivity to what
the receiver is most likely to think of. For this reason,
amongst others, the ability to complete analogies has an
important place in traditional intelligence tests. In other

cases, the rhetorical force of an analogy might be enhanced because a relationship is not immediately retrieved. There is unlikely to be any relation at all between a fish and a bicycle in memory, so 'a fish without a bicycle' cannot be understood as a normal part of the world. However, the analogy forces a search for a relationship. Concluding that a fish has no use for a bicycle at all is a complex but tractable process. The slight difficulty which thus ensues doubtless adds to the force of the analogy. But both examples rely upon an initial primary process, resulting in a mapping of one pair of related items onto another pair, with an 'is like' relationship.

We may now return to the simile and note that it can express a request to compare things which are really quite complicated. For example, the expression 'a bull in a china shop' is a clearly imaginable state of affairs, in which there are many conceivable events, such as the bull charging around, crashing into this and that. The bull is big, powerful, impulsive and unconcerned with its surroundings. Indeed, it cannot conceive of the implications of its natural behaviour. When we say of John in a given circumstance that he behaves like a bull in a china shop, we are inviting people to consider the application of all of the relations between a bull and the china shop to John in his surroundings. The analogy being drawn is thus not restricted to one relationship, but involves many. It is just this feature which gives many similes their full force.

Metaphor is yet another device which draws attention to the likenesses between one thing and another, but this time has all the features of a literal statement, since there is no explicit comparison relationship stated. As a form, they therefore lead to some tricky processing problems. If one encounters 'Adolf Hitler was a butcher', one clearly recognises the statement as being different from the statement 'Adolf Hitler was a painter'. The metaphor is rather like saying that there are certain key aspects of the stereotype of a butcher which are applicable to Hitler. From the point of view of a processor, there is a problem in that the conditions for understanding the truth of a metaphor are different from those for understanding the truth of a literal statement, yet they can have identical forms. There are essentially two ways in which this problem might be overcome. One way is for the processor to treat the statement as literal, and end up by trying to match the *literal* assertion that Hitler was a butcher to facts in memory (primary processing). Because it will not match the facts, it is then taken to be literally false, and so it must be concluded that if the speaker is telling the truth it is a metaphor. Only then will some process of appreciating the metaphor begin. Alternatively, the processor might begin by trying to establish what kind of relationship there is between Hitler and a butcher. Having found a relationship (easy enough) the option exists to find that 'is' is not being used in the manner of a literal assertion. An attractive aspect of this second view is that the discovery that something is a metaphor is not the fundamental part of the understanding process. Given that we process metaphors regularly and often, and do not even notice (see last section of this chapter) it seems likely that this account is along the right lines.[10]

ANALOGIES AS A BASIS FOR UNDERSTANDING

Let us now look at the idea that analogy is an important tool of thinking.[11] The idea is a straightforward extension of the primary-processing principle: If treating situation X as though it were situation Y helps us to think, then map elements of X onto a representation of Y. Let us take a concrete example. Through the work of Kepler, Galileo, and others, we have come to accept the view that the planets of a solar system revolve in nearly circular orbits about the star which is at the centre of the circle. Such a view fits the observed facts of planetary movement. The idea that planets are kept in these orbits by a force—gravity—became incorporated into Newton's picture of how motion can be described. These things are so much a part of our culture that one can assume that most people have some sort of memory structure in which such knowledge is represented, however scantily. By the end of the nineteenth century, modern atomic theory was emerging. It was discovered that rather than being indivisible units, atoms were made up of still smaller particles—electrons, neutrons and protons. One early view of this was that atoms are spheres of protons with electrons embedded inside the sphere (the so-called 'plum pudding' account of the atom). Although this seemed to be a reasonable account of the facts as known in 1898, new evidence forced a change of view, and a new picture emerged: that of electrons circling nuclei which consisted of protons and neutrons. There is obviously a place for an analogy here.

Perhaps the atom is analogous to the solar system. Certainly, there are similarities in the relationships between the entities making up the two things. Thus the distances between the sun and the planets are massive compared to the sizes of the planets and the sun. Similarly, the distances between the nuclei of atoms and the electrons are relatively massive, although the distances by everyday standards are miniscule. Also, the sun exerts a gravitational pull on the planets, and the planets exert a gravitational pull on the sun, while protons exert a pull on electrons and electrons exert a pull on protons. To the extent that a good analogy exists between a solar system and an atom, one can say that a new phenomenon, atomic structure, is *understood* in terms of the old one, solar structure.

It is important to note that an analogy may provide a basis for understanding because the relationships between things which hold in one domain are being applied to another. To the extent that there is a good match, one could say that the analogy is a good one.

Another example of analogy in science concerns the average novice physics student's understanding of electrical circuits. Because of the pedagogical importance of studying how beginners may come to achieve an effective, intuitive and scientifically useful understanding of science, recent years have seen a tremendous surge in systematic studies of these processes. Cognitive scientists are now beginning to unravel some of the characteristics of the individual person's intuitive and technical understanding of a range of phenomena, especially in relation to physics. The work by Gentner and Gentner (see note 11) on electrical circuits is of particular interest here, since it is an extensive treatment of the impact of analogy on reasoning.

In normal everyday descriptions of electrical phenomena, such as a light-bulb coming on when we press a wall switch, we might say something like 'the electrical current flows down one wire, into the bulb, and back out through the other wire. Operating the switch closes a break in one of the wires and lets the electricity flow in this way.'[12] The student who provided this explanation was entirely capable of applying the basic equations of circuits to problems given to him. But what is most interesting is the basic analogy which he was using to make his global description. The analogy is between the flow of water and the flow of 'electricity'. Water is something of which we have a much more basic experience than is electricity. We have visual and tactile experience of it right through our lives from a very early age. And it is a common analogy for electricity even in textbooks. The following statement is typical of many found in elementary textbooks:

Just as the rate of flow of water between two points depends upon the difference of height between them, the rate of flow of electric current between two points depends upon the difference of potential between them.[13]

What this statement shows is an attempt to bring about an understanding of a new relationship, the dependence of electrical current on potential, in terms of something considered to be more familiar, the dependence of the rate of flow of water between two points on the difference in height between the two points. The latter is more familiar, easy to visualise, and provides a framework into which new things can be mapped.

The essence of Gentner and Gentner's argument is this: If people take such an analogy seriously, and use it as a basis for reasoning, the properties of the old domain (water) should afford control over what are imagined to be the properties of the new domain (electricity). That is, thinking about problems in electricity should be done through thinking about what would happen in the water analogy. Quite literally, when operating under this analogy alone, electrical phenomena should be *understood only in terms of water phenomena*. It does not matter that someone using this

analogy 'knows' that water is not electricity. Perhaps all that
they could say on this score is that electricity gives you
shocks, water doesn't, you can see water, you can't see
electricity, etc. But this will not be of much help in understanding how various aspects of electricity relate to one
another. Let us turn to Gentner and Gentner's work to see
the force of the argument.

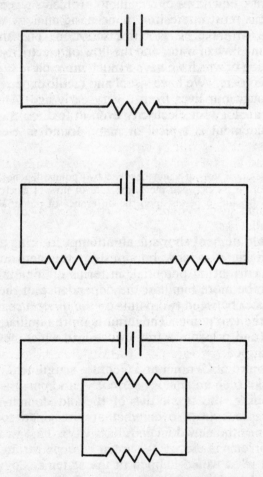

*3.2   Simple circuits of the type studied by Gentner and Gentner. Upper
circuit shows battery at top, and one resistor. Middle circuit is the serial
case; lower circuit the parallel case.*

The kinds of circuit which they investigated are depicted in Figure 3.2. The symbols denote a battery and resistors, connected by wires in various ways. Consider how current flow might depend upon different resistor combinations. First, how is a resistor thought of in terms of the water analogy? Quite simply, a resistor is *a narrowing in a pipe*. By thinking in these terms, a resistor (a constriction) should reduce water flow. Thus, by analogy, a resistor should reduce electrical current, which is correct. Now, what happens if there are two resistors, one after the other (so-called serial combination)? When using the present analogy, people argue that there are two restrictions and so the overall reduction in flow will be greater than with just one. This too happens to be correct when applied to the electrical case. The trouble starts with the parallel case, where in the water analogy people typically stick to the view that there are two constrictions, and that this will offer more 'resistance' than one. Gentner and Gentner found that people concluded that two parallel resistors would lead to reduced current flow over one resistor, which does not accord with reality.[14] Apparently, the water analogy does not offer much in the way of guidance in the parallel case.

One would be justified in attributing these results to just a general failure to understand parallel combinations were it not for the fact that people operating within a different analogical framework produced a different pattern of results. This other framework is the *teeming crowds analogy*, used less frequently in teaching, but none the less used.

In this framework, electricity is considered to be (say) mice running along corridors. Resistors are considered to be gates that only let a few mice through per unit time. We shall restrict ourselves to just these object-mappings. Quite clearly, a single resistor will result in a reduced current flow. With two resistors in series, there are two lots of gates to get through, one after the other, and subjects working with this analogy correctly believed that such a combination would result in a reduced flow. In the case of parallel resistors, subjects reasoned that after the circuit split, there are double the number of gates, and so parallel resistors must lead to *higher* current flow than would be the case with a single resistor (gate). They concluded that parallel resistors result in greater flow than a single resistor, which is not only correct, but stands in complete contrast to the conclusions reached by people working with the water analogy. In a series of structured tests, Gentner and Gentner discovered that when reasoning through the medium of these two analogies, and variants of them, success rates on resistor problems was very different. To complete the picture, they also established that with other types of problems, involving intuitions about battery combinations, the water analogy was superior to the teeming crowds analogy.

This piece of research is interesting for a number of reasons. First of all, it shows that analogy is not just a rather restricted language phenomenon. Rather, it is possible to use an old (or familiar) domain to reason about a new one, even though the objects in the domain do not resemble each other. The simile 'electricity is like water' is an assertion that the relationships between things used in describing the behaviour of water are to some degree applicable to electricity. To take the analogy seriously is to reason about water and apply the result to electricity. Thus analogies allow for reasoning about the new in terms of the old. Another reason why these results are interesting is that they show how an anology creates good predictions sometimes, and bad ones at other times. It is of course a commonplace to speak of 'analogies breaking down', but the problem is that with a brand new domain, the only substitute which we have for primary processing is domain-to-analogy mapping. It is the ony way the new could be related to the familiar. Of course, once an analogical mapping has been established, the next time that a reference is made to the new domain, primary processing should identify in long-term memory the mapped analogical structure, in much the same way as discussed for language understanding and recognising problem-types. Indeed, I would like to conjecture that to the extent that we feel that we understand a new domain, we interpret it analogically. If this is the case, analogy in some form should dominate our conceptual systems, a point to which we shall return shortly.

MODELS, THEORIES, BELIEFS AND REASONING

Quite often when people wish to understand something, they build physical models of what they are trying to understand. Familiar examples include architectural models, which allow people to see what a building will look like, how it will relate to its surroundings, and so on. Wind tunnel models of new aircraft are equally familiar, enabling the designers to assess the aerodynamic properties of their proposals. Children's toys are often models: dolls' houses let the young learn about the relationships between different parts of a house, the different activities which may or may not take place in various rooms, etc.—what the possibilities are. The use of models for the purposes of understanding seems to require little in the way of explanation, yet they serve as the basis for some important observations. The most notable is that models only encapsulate certain aspects of the thing being modelled. A wind tunnel model is not a miniature replica of a full-size aeroplane, it is designed only to capture the shape characteristics of the real thing. Most of the time, when people make models, they are only trying to capture some characteristic which is interesting to them. In this respect, models are the physical counterparts of analogies. And as analogies can be pushed until they break down, so too can physical models. Let us take as a specific example the development of the geologists understanding of rift valleys, where physical models have played a considerable role.

A rift valley is a long strip of country, let down between normal geological faults. A normal fault is a discontinuity between rock strata at an angle approximating a right-angle to the strata. Rifts occur in many parts of the world, and can be so outstanding as to invite conjectures as to their formation from all but the most uninquisitive minds. More than a century ago, one of these great faults, the Rhine Graben, became a subject of serious speculation. The first idea could be summed up by a very simple model. If the stones of an archway are pulled apart, then the keystone (centre stone) will drop. So perhaps the Rhine Graben was produced in this way.

If one thinks about this model, the question arises as to what happened as the keystone went down. With a real keystone, it would just hang down in the arch, but with a rift valley, material under the 'keystone' would have to be displaced. If such displacement took place in a rift valley, the most likely result would have been volcanic activity in the surrounding area. Thus, by taking the model seriously, a prediction based on it could be made. The lack of evidence of volcanic activity showed that the 'keystone' model was flawed.[15] In 1939, the geologist Hans Cloos[16] published a paper in which he reported findings with purpose-made physical models. Layers of moist clay were placed on two boards, and the boards were pulled apart very slowly. The result showed inclined tearing, characteristic of rift valleys. However, there are other more subtle aspects of rifts, one of which is that the adjoining areas show an upwards inclination towards the rift itself, known as horsts. This was not captured in Cloos' first model. Incorporating the pull principle, Cloos produced another physical model which had a single board, flat under the clay layers. The board was pushed slowly upward in the middle so that it arched beneath the clay layers. By pushing in this way, there was a stretching, particularly of the top layers of the clay. This brought about a simulation of rifting and dropping, while the uplift and horsts of the surrounding area were also produced. Thus his model showed how a suitable upthrust could replace the original pull idea.

Taking the upthrust principle as being the likely explanation of rifting, Cloos went on to consider what would happen in a case where the upthrust had boundaries, in order to reproduce yet more of the naturally occurring geological phenomena. An oval hot water bottle was covered with moist clay. It was then slowly filled with water, producing a maximal upthrust in the centre, and no upthrust at the edges. The result is not only the production of a primary rift in the middle, but also splitting of the rift towards the edges. This splaying out (bifurcation) is observed in the Rhine Graben, and other rift valleys like the Red Sea.

These models show how physical analogies can help in developing an understanding of rift valley formation. Perhaps the reader feels that he or she actually understands something more about rift valleys than they did before, although the purpose here is not to talk about geology! The purpose is to show how physical models, like analogies, enable the sort of 'mental tinkering' to take place which brings about understanding itself.

The next step in our argument is the introduction of the idea of a mental model rather than a physical one. Let us simply assert that people understand things and reason about things by using mental models, and try to put some flesh on this very skeletal notion. A mental model is that set of representations which is used in drawing a conclusion about something, in going beyond the evidence given. In our discussion of primary processing, it was shown how existing memory structures were used to interpret language input. When analogies were introduced, it was suggested that an old domain can be used as memory structure onto which the elements of a new domain might be mapped, after the fashion of primary processing. After an analogy has been used a few times, the mapping should be well established, and future references to the new domain should call up the entire mapped structure, in the fashion of primary processing. What these mappings do is to provide a *set of constraints* on what can happen next. Just as it is the case that a physical set-up can constrain the possible things that can be done with a physical model, so it is the case with memory mappings. Recall the strange example of the three cups problem. Making a very simple mapping leads to a strong feeling of understanding, and does not allow enough possibilities to be able to solve the problem properly. And again, just as with physical models, novel outcomes are possible within the confines of the basic model. We can characterise a mental model thus: It is a set of conceptions being applied to a current situation which lead to a restricted set of terms through which the current situation can be understood or thought about. In the chapters which follow, the impact of this line of reasoning will be made clear. Not only does a mental model provide a domain for thinking in, it also rules out other ways of thinking.

This final point actually opens up a hornets' nest. Surely, you might say, while one might use the water analogy (say) in reasoning about electricity, one need not *believe* that this is the only way, the right way, or anything else leading to a commitment of a serious kind. At one extreme, this argument is quite right. When confronted with a new analogy that is explicitly stated as an analogy, there is no reason to be committed to believing that it is any good, or that it covers all of the facts. Indeed, in retrospect, it is easy to see how an analogy has failed. To accommodate this possibility, let us say that when an old domain of knowledge is used as a model for a new domain, we are entertaining a *conjecture* that the first explains the second. Suppose that the analogy holds good, and that more and more of the new domain is predicted on the basis of the old. Retaining some scepticism, we may now allow that we are holding the *theory* that the first explains the second, though by now the analogical aspect may have become heavily annotated with caveats about 'differences', and the original analogy may appear to be less significant as a constraint on thinking. The question now arises as to what alternatives we are considering. If we do not have any alternatives, we may say things like this: 'To the extent that I understand this, . . .' where the dots will be some detailed description based on analogy. If you do have alternatives, you may say: 'Yes, I understand it, it is either like this . . . or this . . ., there seem to be two alternatives'. If the two models agree sufficiently well, and you can tie enough of the facts together, people may even give you credit for understanding something! You would be in the position of someone who had to admit that there were alternative theories about the domain in question. The problem is that there is no way of knowing how many *other* possibilities there are, and the more time one spends scrutinising one model, the less likely one is to consider seriously any other. And so you may come to believe the mapping for all practical purposes. Indeed, after explaining a particularly difficult and very general-purpose theory in physics, an eminent scientist was asked whether he had considered any other ways of looking at the problem. He simply stated that he had enough trouble exploring *one* way of looking at the problem!

While few of us are concerned with the intricacies of modern physics, on the view being built up here, the same arguments can be applied to the way we view many of the problems of everyday life. The hard fact is that to review even a few alternatives takes time, and considering the number of things that we have to understand, it is scarcely surprising if one does not consider even a small number of plausible alternatives. In many everyday situations, primary processing presents us with a starting point for reasoning, a point which is restricting, but which is probably one which often we do not get far beyond. This will be the substance of the next chapter.

METAPHORS ARE UBIQUITOUS AND INSIDIOUS

Usually, one thinks of a metaphor as being a special-purpose device of rhetoric. The arguments presented above show how analogies can become serious models used in understanding, rather than being mere literary devices. We shall now consider those kinds of metaphor which are so commonplace in our everyday language that we scarcely think of them as metaphors at all. They are now such a part of our thinking (understanding) that we appear to treat them as though they were expressions with literal meanings. The main point is that through these 'mundane metaphors' we restrict ourselves to seeing the world in certain ways, just as with new analogies we might commit ourselves to a particular picture of the world.

First, to illustrate what I mean by 'mundane metaphors', I shall contrast two examples with two examples of novel metaphors and two examples of 'frozen' metaphors, i.e. metaphors which have simply become idioms inexplicable to all but the historical linguist:

Novel Metaphors:
Robins are the knight-crusaders of the bird world.

> The Sundays of man's life,
> Threaded together on time's string,
> Make bracelets to adorn the wife
> Of the eternal glorious kind.

Frozen Metaphors:
> John kicked the bucket.
> When he gets back from the disco, Martin has had his chips.

Mundane Metaphors:
> I cannot see the point of your argument.
> Louise is on top of her homework now.

The first two are plainly of a literary variety. Everyone knows what the next two mean, though few will know why these curious expressions came to denote dying and being in severe trouble (even being killed) respectively, although they both have origins in novel metaphor. They have simply become idioms of the language. But the mundane metaphors are somewhat different, since they belong to elaborate and extensive systems of conceptual mappings.

Following on from a steady trickle of work on the role metaphors play in our understanding, linguistic philosophers, George Lakoff and Mark Johnson,[17] carried out a rather thorough scan of the occurrence of what we are calling mundane metaphors. These investigators show through the medium of numerous examples just how ubiquitous such metaphors are, and attempt an interesting grouping of them into families. Some of these families are as follows. Arguments (scientific or hot domestic ones) are seen as war, and include things like 'You'll never win your argument', 'All of my arguments were shot down', 'This view is full of weak points', and so on. Another example is two classes of metaphor used to talk about the mind. 'I'm a little rusty today', 'He broke down', 'His mind doesn't work properly under examination conditions' are all examples of what Lakoff and Johnson call the *mind is a machine* metaphor. In contrast, the other main metaphor for mind is *mind is a brittle object*, having as exemplars things like 'She is easily crushed', 'Sheena says we are all cracking up', and 'He found the experience shattering'.

A particularly pervasive set of metaphors relate to spatial expressions. 'I'm on top of the world today', and 'Last week I was feeling really low', illustrate the seemingly natural relation between being up and down, and being happy or sad, capable or incapable. In fact, there are many varieties of these orientational metaphors. *More* is up and *less* is down: 'The number of students studying programming goes up each year', 'Turn the record player down'. *Having control* is up, and *being subject to control* is down. 'He is in a superior position in the firm', 'My children are under my control', 'The faculty administrators are getting on top of me'. These are all natural turns of phrase for us, all 'mundane' metaphors. Yet metaphors they are.

Lakoff and Johnson studied many other examples, and provide a fascinating analysis of the interrelations between metaphors. Up–down metaphors have in fact received a fair amount of attention, and are especially interesting because it is possible to speculate about their origins in physical and social experience. Thus *having control is up* may come from a primitive origin in that physical size is correlated with physical strength, and being above someone in a fight usually accords an advantage. Which is the real basis is a matter for speculation. *Happy is up*, *sad down* may have a physical basis in the typical postures adopted during happiness and elation versus sadness and depression. *More is up and less is down* may have an experiential basis in the manipulation of materials in the world. If one makes a pile of something, the more one adds, on the whole, the higher the pile. The more rain falls into a river, the higher the level of the water.[18] These putative physical origins at least smack of plausibility, although a means of establishing exactly how such ubiquitous metaphors actually originate remains to be discovered.

Each of the metaphorical underpinnings of the concepts illustrated above are the result of mapping a new domain onto an old one at some point. Although we may now think of mappings into the terms up–down as arbitrary, if Lakoff and Johnson are right, then what now appears arbitrary must have evolved through quite novel mappings in which one domain was seen as a vehicle for expressing another. And the strong implication is that these mappings were between new things (e.g. expressing one's state of mind linguistically) and some familiar physical thing, such as posture or positional advantage in a fight.

Other basic or primitive aspects of life provide yet other fields of daily metaphors. The familiar *journey* provides a basis for many more abstract things. Thus Lakoff and Johnson identify *an argument is a journey* ('at last we seem to be getting near to the conclusion', 'we have set out to prove that much of language is metaphoric'), and *human relationships are a journey* ('this relationship is at a dead end'). Journeys are familiar to everyone, and provide a rich knowledge-base on which rich analogical models can be based.

There are several aspects of this work which are of great significance. Perhaps one of the most important is that mappings between new situations and familiar, physically basic situations like fights, power struggles, journeys, and a host of other familiar situations are made very easily, almost unnoticed. This aspect of primary processing has received scant attention, but there can be little doubt that it does happen all of the time, and seldom goes noticed. This leads us to a second point, and that is that once a mapping has been adopted, it specifies the model with which we think, and if we are uncritical of it, it is the basis of our entire outlook on things. In this sense, metaphors are insidious. A simple example is the contrast between *argument as war* and *argument as a journey*. The entailments of the former include gaining ground at the expense of an adversary, while the latter have entailments of exploration and discovery. Living by the argument is war metaphor is to have a very different attitude towards others than is living by the argument is a journey metaphor. And as Lakoff and Johnson point out, other metaphors go hand in hand with still other ways of looking at things. For instance, if argument was to be thought of as a work of art, then interpersonal communications could take on a very different complexion.

One final example. Many things require action, and are frequently thought of in terms of war ('Let battle commence'). Lakoff and Johnson cite the one-time President of the USA, Jimmy Carter, as reacting to the energy crisis by declaring 'the moral equivalent of war'. As they point out, this opens up a whole range of analogues of war-related acts, like there being an enemy, setting targets, imposing sanctions, calling for sacrifice, and so on, leading through inference to there being a hostile foreign enemy, and a need to fight for survival. Other metaphors are more conducive to more flexible views of energy sources, which do not entail fighting over diminishing resources. Yet in the USA, as in most of the world, the louder voices of the politicians led to an imposition of their metaphors. But our main point is that the metaphors people use set the tracks along which thoughts and beliefs will tend to run. Language restricts thoughts just as thoughts manifest in language.

IN CONCLUSION

Our aim has been to extend the principles of interpretation described in the last chapter, and to show something of their generality. This we have done in two ways. First, working on a problem depends critically on having a mental representation to manipulate. To the extent that encountering a problem leads to the identification of a suitable background knowledge structure in long-term memory, the problem can be mapped into this structure. On the basis of this structure, operations can be carried out which lead towards a solution. If a sufficiently relevant structure is not activated, two things can happen. If the structure is inappropriate, it will not lead to an answer, because the understanding itself will not be appropriate. If the structure is too limited, a compelling feeling of understanding may come about, but one's conception of the problem will be inappropriately narrow, and will almost certainly lead to error.

These extensions of primary processing are fairly straightforward, relying on the mapping of a problem description onto a memory structure which is really just a fuller description of that type of problem, thus allowing inferences to be drawn from its entailments. But all of our understanding cannot be of this simple type, since we learn to appreciate completely new things. Part of the evidence for this comes from work on metaphor. It had long been supposed that these language devices were the tip of an iceberg, the surface manifestations of underlying thought processes. Indeed, the recent research on analogical thinking vindicates such a point of view. People can and do think about a new domain by making predictions from an older more familiar domain. This can lead both to results which correspond to observable reality in the new domain, and to results which are at loggerheads to it, as beautifully illustrated in the work of Gentner and Gentner. It is suggested that once an analogy becomes accepted as an appropriate way of looking at some new phenomenon, it progresses from conjecture through theory to belief. And the explorations which are enabled by analogical reasoning, and testing the 'fit' of an analogy constitute a growth of real understanding. Indeed, analogical reasoning is best thought of as using an old domain as a *'mental model'* of a new domain. Just as with physical models one can explore the properties of the model to test ideas about what happens in the real world, so it is with mental models, except that they are representations in the head rather than in the outside world. Indeed, any situational representation can serve as a model, be it a 'script' or some structured knowledge introduced by analogy.

Finally, if the interpretation of the new in terms of the old is as prevalent as this view would lead one to suppose, then one would expect everyday language to be full of metaphor. The 'mundane metaphors' discussed in the last section show this to be the case. Indeed, Lakoff and Johnson have performed a service to the entire study of meaning by exploring a wide range of apparently fundamental metaphors, and carefully investigating their entailment patterns. They conclude, in consonance with our discussions of primary processing, that mundane and novel metaphors not only serve to give a foundation to understanding, but that by adopting particular ones without scrutiny, other ways of looking at things are squeezed out.

CHAPTER 4

Intuition and Heuristics

In this chapter I shall introduce a range of issues associated with intuitive thinking. Intuitive thinking is not particularly easy to define, but it is well worth examining some of the conditions under which the term 'intuitive' is used. Perhaps the dominant use of the expression contrasts in most people's minds with careful reasoning in which all of the pros and cons of an argument or situation are carefully and, if possible, exhaustively evaluated. Intuitive reasoning is thus informal, based on the 'feel' of a situation. In many ways it is quick and dirty, requiring less time than more analytic thinking. Another use of the term is found when we say of an assertion 'that's intuitively obvious', or 'that fits my intuitions'. We say that someone has good intuitions if what they say seems to be based on little analytic thinking, yet turns out to fit the facts.

Certain people give a somewhat magical status to the idea of intuition. There are mystiques surrounding the power of intuition in women, in cowboy lore, in the native Indian populations of many countries. Readers of the Tarot and crystal balls make frequent references to their intuition. Intuitions are seen as powers and as commodities in these and other settings, and can become swathed in mystery. Some people are said in daily life to have better intuitions than others, some scientists are said to have better 'intuitive grasps' of their subjects.

Our aim is to examine some of the facts of everyday intuition, and to try to do so within the framework of information processing used up to now. So what of the more seemingly ethereal uses of the term? It is entirely possible for someone to have a strong view about something, perhaps a view which turns out to match reality rather well, without being able to justify it to any great extent, and certainly without being able to verbalise an entire chain of logical argument. We can feel sure about things without being able to say why. The problem from an information-processing point of view is to say how these states of mind come about. I am going to suggest a very simple starting point. The intuitive acceptability of something depends upon the readiness with which primary processing finds a suitable representation in memory which could be used to interpret the input. A simple example will illustrate the idea. It is intuitive that a fair coin tossed once is just as likely to come down heads as it is to be tails. It is intuitive that if a coin is tossed a large number of times the number of heads and the number of tails will be approximately equal. This is because there is a good match between the situation and people's conceptions of a fair coin, and these simple expectations are correct. It is also intuitive that if a fair coin is tossed five times and comes out heads each time that the most likely outcome next time will be *tails*. Yet this is entirely wrong. It is a misconception called the 'gambler's fallacy'. Most people have this intuition, yet think of what it means. If it were true, it would mean that only on the very first time a coin was ever tossed is it the case that the odds on heads or tails are definitionally even!

When a match is found between a state of the world and a structure in memory, we have the minimum grounds for a number of cognitive activities. We can think about the state of the world in terms of the model in more or less detail, more or less exhaustively. Or we can do very little work and just use the results of some cursory processing to say something about the state of the world. I wish to equate part of the meaning of intuition with this brief, shallow processing based upon mappings onto memory structures, and return to other aspects at a later point.

THE QUICK AND DIRTY APPROACH: COGNITIVE HEURISTICS

Thinking of any sort takes time, and the more detailed the thinking, the longer the time taken. We are always faced with numerous things to try to understand; indeed, anything about which we venture an opinion or make a statement is hopefully something which we understand. But the depth and carefulness of our understanding cannot be uniform because of the time constraint. So it is hardly surprising if there are mental procedures which are fast but incomplete. This *time constraint* is not the only major factor which might prevent extensive and deep thinking. We are frequently subject to *data constraint*. Data constraint means that all of the pertinent facts may not be available to us when we are forced to make a judgement, or to attempt to understand things. Take a simple everyday problem like deciding which washing machine to buy. To make a rational decision, it is necessary to have all price data, all reliability data, cost of all parts, proximity of repair-centres, average delay at call-out for repairs, even the stability and medium-term prospects of the manufacturers! This list is not complete, of course, but even if it were, it would be something of a nightmare trying to work out an optimum choice on the basis of so much data. So although data-constraint is a problem with high data-loads, it is likely that the time constraint would get in the way of using the data. Finally, as the problem of combining the evidence shown above illustrates, one is likely to encounter a *skill constraint*: few people are likely to be able to find an optimal solution given complex data.

Obviously, in order to be able to make decisions at all, some simplifying procedures are called for, otherwise we would spend all of our time locked in our thoughts! Such procedures are called 'heuristics', from the Greek word for 'steersman'. Heuristics are procedures which are valuable for getting a solution, but the solution is not guaranteed to be the optimal one. There is no way of proving that if the procedure is followed, the desired outcome will follow. In the language of procedures, heuristics contrast with *algorithms*,[1] which specify actions guaranteed to produce the desired outcome. Just because heuristics do not carry a guarantee does not mean they are random. Rather, they are rules of thumb which work most of the time. There is evidence of mental procedures of just this sort, and ample demonstration of situations where they are used. Let us look at two of these, extensively investigated by the psychologists, Amos Tversky and Daniel Kahneman,[2] who have been particularly instrumental in bringing heuristic reasoning to the attention of psychologists.

Suppose that you are judging which make of washing machine, A or B, is more reliable, because your friend has made a spur of the moment decision to buy one. You might do this by thinking of evidence, things you have seen or read or experienced, favouring A or B. Such a procedure of utilising memory search for relevant examples, is called 'judgement by availability', since it relies upon how available pertinent data are in memory. It is useful because it is generally the case that things which are more numerous will be more available to memory.[3] So if you have encountered more bad comments about A than B, then you are likely to remember more bad comments about A, which is a valuable basis for giving advice.

However, things can go wrong with this heuristic, because other factors influence ease of retrieval. Recent events are recalled more readily than earlier events,[4] and significant events are recalled more readily. Thus if your own washing machine (B) broke down recently involving you in considerable domestic havoc, this will cetainly be the first thing to spring to mind. A recent personal experience can thus dominate the availability pattern, even if you were just unlucky with your own particular machine.[5]

If a number of pertinent events have occurred together in a limited period, more *familiar* events are more available than less familiar things. This is probably because more familiar things produce rich memory mappings (through primary processing) while less familiar things map into little if anything.[6] An experiment by Tversky and Kahneman[7] shows how memory influences judgement. Subjects had to read lists of people's names, some very famous, some less so. In one case there were fewer women's names than men's, but the women were more famous. In the other case, there were fewer men, but this time *they* were more famous. One group of subjects carried out a full-scale recall of all the names, and recalled famous people more easily. Another group made a quick judgement as to whether more women's or men's names appeared in the lists. If the list contained more famous women, subjects thought that there were more women. The same applied *mutatis mutandis* for the famous men case.

This heuristic has been invoked as a plausible explanation of a number of more socially significant phenomena. For instance, it is a commonplace that if two people are jointly responsible for a venture, then each of them is prone to suppose that he is involved more than the other. It is common in the office, at home, and on the sports field. Experimental studies of this phenomenon have been carried out[8] investigating married couples and supervisor–student pairs. In each case, each member of the pair was asked to indicate the proportion of time and effort which they and their partner put into a variety of tasks. In all cases, each partner thought that he or she put in more effort and time than the partner. Since this results in a logically impossible situation overall, it follows that each partner overestimates his own contribution. It is interesting to note that the pattern of overestimation applied to situations where there were actually negative (undesirable) outcomes, so the results are unlikely to reflect a misguided attempt to impress the experimenter! Finally, when subjects were requested to list the contributions of themselves and the other, each gave more examples of their own contributions. This bias of egocentricity is explicable in terms of availability, at least in part. The memory results themselves are unsurprising, since it is well established that people remember events that they relate directly to themselves better than other events. But the availability of this information to memory clearly leads to a distortion in the attribution of responsibility to oneself and one's partner.

Availability is important whenever judgements are based on the ease of retrieving examples. Thus, Kahneman and Tversky have shown that people's estimates of how many examples there are in a given category (such as flowers, or Russian novelists) actually correlates fairly well with the number they can think of if asked to make a list over a two-minute period. Thus how quickly a very few examples can be thought of is a function of how many are ultimately available. However, there are some cases where it is difficult to think of examples although there are many of them. For instance, in English, is it more likely that there are more words starting with the letter 'k' or with the letter 'k' in the third position? There is a bias towards believing that there are more in the first position (over a set of letters, the ratio is about 2:1). This is because of the mechanisms of memory retrieval. It is easier to think of examples of words beginning with a particular letter than it is to think of examples with the letter in the middle, on the whole.[9] Of course, it is not the case that all letters are more frequently used to head a word than they are used in the third position.

A close relative of memory-based availability is availability to imagination. Some things are simply easier to construct in the imagination than others. For instance, imagine that a group of ten people wish to form a committee of two people. They argue about who should be on it, and conclude that if they are going to have a committee, more of the ten should be represented. They decide upon eight. Will there be more combinations of two people to consider as the possible constitution than there would with eight? Think about it.[10] In fact, there are exactly the same number of combinations, because with 8 members there are 2 non-members, and with 2 members there are 8 non-members. But if you are like most people, and try to work it out by trying a few examples, because it is easier to think of new combinations of 2 than it is of 8, you will likely have thought that there are more committees of 2 than there are of 8. In fact, Kahneman and Tversky show estimates of the number of committees goes down with an increasing number of would-be members.

Availability, either from memory or by constructing examples, seems to be a pervasive factor in making many kinds of judgement and decision. As a heuristic it is broadly effective, but can lead to some quite profound errors of judgement. The second heuristic goes by the somewhat cumbersome label of *representativeness*, and is very closely related to primary processing in that it relies upon matching descriptions or states of the world onto representations in memory. It is to this that we shall now turn.

Representativeness and Primary Processing

Suppose that you hear of some of the attributes of a person—call him Fred Smith. Fred Smith was very good at mathematical subjects at school, but was generally weak at history, literature and other arts. He is generally considered by those who know him as something of a cold fish, and is really rather introverted. On the basis of this, would you consider it more likely that Fred is a chef at a London restaurant, or an accountant? In the absence of any other information, most people would guess that he is an accountant. There is little more to do than assess the similarity of the character description to representations in long-term memory of what each job stereotype is likely to be. The character description is being judged as more or less representative of two models (character stereotypes).

Notice that representativeness gives a foundation for judgements of probability and likelihood, judgements which we make frequently in our daily lives. Indeed, some of the most interesting work on this heuristic has come from studies of people's judgements of probability. Thus Tversky and Kahneman[11] asked people to give judgements about the relative probabilities of finding exact birth orders in samples of families. One such problem said that there was a survey of all families with six children comprising three girls and three boys in a particular area. Which exact birth order is more likely, BBBGGG or GBGBBG? Most people think that the latter is very much more likely. Why? Because it is representative of the randomness underlying whether a child is born a boy or a girl. This is essentially wrong. The probabilities of getting these two exact birth orders are very very close to identical. But the mapping between the properties of the second sequence and intuitive models of randomness is very good. We might suppose that people have the following sort of data in their memory-structures about birth order:

- On any occasion when a child is born, it is random whether it is a boy or a girl.

And their concept of random will include this:

- Randomness is when the data do not fit any obvious rule.

Well, BBBGGG is a pattern which could have been generated by a rule rather than by a random process, while GBGBBG is not. So the second pattern is more representative. In fact, a random process would generate both sequences with equal likelihood, along with other equally likely sequences like GGGBBB and BGBGGB and BGBGBG, etc.

In passing, it is worth noting a third candidate for a rule in relation to birth order:

- The number of boys and of girls born will be about equal in the long run.

This too can lead to problems. Some people believe that the exact birth sequence BB is less likely than BG, for instance, because BB seems to be less representative of the rule. This problem is accentuated when one considers that the exact orders BBBBB and GBGGB are equally likely as well![12]

A particularly striking example of the kinds of fallacy which can result from the sensible application of representativeness is the conjunction error (Tversky and Kahneman).[13] The following character sketch comes from one of their examples:

- Linda is 31 years old, single, outspoken and very bright. She majored in philosophy. As a student, she was very concerned with issues of social discrimination and justice, and also participated in anti-nuclear demonstrations.

Respondents were asked which was more likely, that Linda is a bank-teller or that she is a bank-teller who is active in the feminist movement. The majority of the respondents thought the latter more likely. This seems reasonable, since her background makes it most likely that she would be involved in movements of social significance. Yet the response is strictly speaking illogical. She cannot be a bank-teller interested in feminism without first being a bank-teller. She must be *as likely* to be a bank-teller, or more likely. This clash between representativeness and logic holds up under very strictly controlled conditions of testing, and cannot be easily explained away.

The representative heuristic is of major significance for human judgement. It is closely related to primary processing, which we have seen at the root of much of our understanding. We make judgements of the likelihood of things on the basis of the correspondence between the data and the model. This is a very useful and powerful heuristic which sometimes leads us astray.

Another aspect of representativeness relates to causality, also discussed by Kahneman and Tversky. An outcome can be thought of as typical or not typical of some particular process. For instance, when trying to start a car on a cold winter's morning, the engine may not turn over properly. This is a typical outcome of the behaviour of batteries in low temperatures, although there could possibly be some other reason for the car's behaviour, like a faulty circuit.

The tendency to think in terms of causes can be nicely illustrated by the following example: In which would you have more confidence, the prediction of a man's height from his weight, or vice versa. Most people would say 'vice versa', presumably because the prototype tall man is heavier than the prototype short man, arguing from representativeness and some idea that height 'causes' weight. Of course, in reality, weight predicts height just as well as height predicts weight. The strong intuitions produced by representativeness can lead to some inappropriate judgements.

PUTTING TOGETHER EVIDENCE

In our daily lives, we do not always feel committed to an opinion, but feel that new evidence might make us change our minds. Suppose that a murder has been committed, and there are two possible culprits, Mr Andrews and Mr Brown. You already know that Andrews has a criminal record, and that Brown does not. At this point, you might believe that Andrews is more likely to have perpetrated the murder. You might even be prepared to say that the odds are 2:1 that Andrews did it. Later on, you find that Brown was near the scene of the crime, and has a lot of enemies in a somewhat shady business world. At this point, you might well revise your opinion such that you say the odds favour Brown as the culprit.

In any revision process, there are two elements (at least)

to be *combined*: the prior odds, which are based on the first bits of data, and the new odds given the new bits of data. Doing this is quite a problem for human beings, as we shall see, because it is necessary to give a weighting to both pieces of evidence, and then combine them in some way. Now there is a procedure from the theory of probability which specifies a means of combining old odds (called prior odds) and new evidence (called the likelihood ratio). This principle, known as Bayes' theorem after its discoverer,[14] states in its simplest form that:

NEW ODDS = PRIOR ODDS × LIKELIHOOD RATIO

So if the first bit of evidence favoured Mr Andrews with a likelihood of 2:1, and the new bit (alone) was only, say, 1:5 in favour of Andrews (i.e. it actually favours Brown), then the new odds in favour of Andrews would be:

$$2/1 \times 1/5 = 2/5$$

i.e. the odds are now 5:2 that Brown did it.

Now of course, people do not usually go around revising odds in this way, but it would be good if people somehow conformed to such a principle. In fact, in situations where people are presented with explicit tasks of revision, given numbers to work from, they do revise odds in the right direction, but tend to underestimate the impact of new evidence compared with the expected Bayesian outcome.[15]

Things can be very different when the task is not one of explicit revision, as various researchers have discovered. The following example comes once again from the extensive research of Kahneman and Tversky.[16] They told a group of subjects that an individual had been chosen from a group consisting of 70 engineers and 30 lawyers, and provided a brief character sketch:

● Dick is a 30-year-old man, married, with no children. A man of high ability and high motivation, he is likely to be quite successful in his field. He is well liked by his colleagues.

Is Dick likely to be an engineer, a lawyer, or equally likely to be either? Looking at the character-sketch makes it easy to understand the predominant response: 'even odds', or words to that effect. But of course it is *not* even odds. The character-sketch contains no information which maps onto any discriminating aspect of lawyer or engineer stereotypes, so the odds from this are indeed 50:50. But Dick was selected from a pool of *70* engineers and only *30* lawyers, so he is more likely to be an engineer. The odds are $7/3 \times 50/50 = 7/3$ in favour of his being an engineer. What seems to have happened is that subjects allow the representativeness heuristic to dominate their judgements so as to exclude evidence integration. Such effects are pervasive and very compelling indeed, and of the greatest importance. The psychologist Max Hammerton [17] has demonstrated the same failure to take base rate into account in situations where diagnosis of cancer is at issue. Given a test which has a 95 per cent chance of detecting cancer if it is there, and a 5 per cent chance of falsely detecting it if it is not there, how would you feel if your scan result came out positive? Most people believe that the chances that they have cancer would be 95 per cent. Given that the base rate (i.e. the chance of a person in the population having this sort of cancer) is, say, 1 in 10,000, the actual likelihood of your having it given a positive outcome is really 0.0019, which, while bad enough, is nothing like 0.95! It is doubtless the case that humans find it much easier to think about one of a few concrete situations rather than about abstractions like 'base rate', as ample evidence demonstrates.[18] Just why is an intriguing psychological mystery, but there are some leaders in the literature.

One possibility is that people find it easier to think in terms of causes and effects. In the engineer–lawyer case given earlier, one would not say that because there were 70 per cent engineers, this causes Dick to be an engineer with 70 per cent certainty. On the other hand, being an engineer might be the 'cause' (strictly, reason) for his carrying a slide-rule everywhere. In a very interesting set of studies, Kahneman and Tversky[19] showed how causality seems to influence the combination of evidence. Thus, scenes were described in which an accident occurred involving a taxi-cab which could be one of two colours. A hypothetical witness said he thought it was one colour, and an eyesight test showed that the witness was 70 per cent reliable. Given information like '30 per cent of the cabs in the town were green', subjects failed to use this information in making a judgement in the face of all the evidence. However, if told '30 per cent of cab accidents involve green cabs', they did tend to incorporate the information. The second way of putting it provides a causal link between cab colour and the likelihood of having an accident.

It is not just representativeness which causes problems with evidence integration. If evidence is presented sequentially, memory can affect the chances of ending up with a balanced point of view. Not only is more recently presented evidence more likely to be available during subsequent deliberation, but it is more likely to be the current focus of attention. This makes it extremely likely that more recent evidence will weigh more heavily than earlier evidence. In a startling test of what this might imply, 'courtroom' evidence was presented to groups of people in different orders. A variety of tests showed that the weight of evidence in favour of one or other of two protagonists was heavily influenced by recency. The most recent evidence was given more weight by judges in assessing guilt or innocence. [20]

ARE PEOPLE TOO CONFIDENT ABOUT THINGS?

We have varying degrees of confidence about things, and have a whole armoury of words to signal confidence to others. 'I'm sure/not sure/fairly positive/certain' 'My guess is/it's usually the case that/I'm just guessing . . .' and so on. The validity of our confidence, both to ourselves and as expressed to other people, is of the greatest importance. Yet we are frequently faced with situations where a high degree of confidence is *felt*, but which may not be easy to justify rationally. This is particularly and necessarily true of heuristic reasoning which characterises intuition.

Let us begin with some studies directed at the confidence which people express about the correctness of their own knowledge, as thoroughly explored by Slovic, Fischhoff and others. [21] The typical paradigm of such studies has been to ask people to make 'difficult' judgements involving incomplete knowledge. A typical judgement might be to decide whether the following statement is true or false, expressing confidence on a scale of 0 (sure false) through 0.5 (pure guess) to 1 (sure true):

Absinthe is an island in the Caribbean.

The questions can be set at various levels of difficulty, but a pervasive finding is that subjects consistently assign higher ratings of confidence than is justified by actual performance over a series of trails. For instance, if their average performance is 70 per cent correct over a series, average confidence might be 80–85 per cent. People are *overconfident* in such situations. It is important to realise that this is not a trivial phenomenon. It is important in many decision-making settings, business, financial, military, and so on. While experts in some fields are 'well-calibrated', in that their confidence reflects likely outcomes (an example being weather judgements), in relatively novel settings the problem is rife, and has given rise to attempts to train people to be better calibrated. Certainly, in the laboratory, the difficulty of inducing changes seems to be easily demonstrated. When shown the kinds of error they make, subjects still do not move their estimates any closer to objective levels which they will finally achieve. They can even be induced to make bets, after being informed, and *still* subjects do not make the appropriate adjustments. If overconfidence was simply due to uncertainty about using numbers, then some adjustment would be expected. Rather, it looks as if the excessive confidence results from a misguided belief in one's ability to judge certainty.

What does appear to cause a change in the direction of conservatism, and hence a closer approximation to the objective frequency of correct responses, is to force a change in the decision procedure which people seem to use. If subjects are invited to write down their reasons for or against the choice they finally make, they find it very much easier to write down the reasons *for*.[22] Subjects writing down only reasons *against* a choice produce far less, and take longer to produce what they do write down. Now there is nothing logically necessary about this: even if one has an equal number of reasons for and against, those against could be judged less critical, and given a lower weight in the balance of the decision. Rather, it appears to be the case that once a particular alternative is favoured, it is *easier to think of evidence consistent with that alternative, on the whole*. So the whole process of coming to a decision develops a positive feedback characteristic in which the initial route finds more and more consistent evidence in memory. Certainly, if subjects are requested to write down only reasons against, then confidence *does* drop, and performance comes closer to realistic calibration.

The account given above serves as the basis for a possible process model. Consider the problem of deciding the truth or falsity of 'Absinthe is a Caribbean island'. A subject might begin by checking in memory for relationships between Absinthe and Caribbean islands. They may find that Absinthe is a drink, so is Curacao. They may have an idea that Curacao is an island somewhere in the Caribbean. They may suspect that it is French-speaking. Absinthe is a French drink—remember the painting 'The Absinthe Drinker', that's French. Notice how all of the data produced by this search, although uncertain, revolve around an assessment of the plausibility of the hypothesis.

Perhaps one of the most dramatic of the overconfidence phenomena is hindsight. We are all familiar with this irritating phenomenon: A spouse or a colleague says, 'I told you so' or 'I knew that would happen' when some event did not conform to our predictions. Apart from the minor battering which one's ego might take, one might feel that the other person's confidence in what they 'knew all along' is unjustified. Now of course, sometimes their prior judgements might have been better than ours, especially if they were better informed. But one never knows for sure.

A hindsight situation is one in which a claim is made in retrospect about one's likelihood judgement of a particular outcome, as though one did not know the outcome, but when in fact one does. In the laboratory it is an easy matter to demonstrate that such judgements yield inflated levels of confidence when compared to truly prior judgements. In a series of beautiful investigations, Fischhoff and his colleagues[23] had subjects judge the probability of difficult propositions like the 'absinthe' example discussed above. However, one group of subjects had the correct response circled, so that

they *knew* what the correct response was. They had to indicate *what they would have put if they did not already know
the answer*. The confidence levels were higher in this group
than in the truly prior group which did not see the answer
circled.

It might well be objected that there was no need for the
hindsight group to tell the truth. They could afford to fool
the experimenter into thinking that they were better informed than was in fact the case. However, another condition ruled out this explanation. The investigators *retested*
the subjects who did not know the answers at the time of
testing, after a delay. This time, they got items which were
now circled as correct. The new knowledge of the correct
answers had a profound effect upon subjects' memories of
how they had responded before. First, they tended to remember ticking off the correct answer more often than they
should. Secondly, when they *correctly* remembered ticking
off the correct answer, they *incorrectly* remembered being
more confident than they actually were! Since neither feedback nor monetary incentive had much effect on these ten-
dencies, it is not the case that subjects are lying to save face.
Hindsight is a genuine distortion of judgement and confidence, and also distorts memory.

CONFIDENCE, INTUITION AND UNDERSTANDING

Hindsight is not just an irritating social phenomenon. It is
built into human thinking and has a profound effect on the
way in which we understand the world. The generality of the
phenomenon is readily established in quite different situations. One such study introduced a group of students to a
hypothetical experiment on rat behaviour.[24] The experiment
was described, and two possible outcomes were suggested.
Subjects were then invited to judge which would be the most
likely outcome, and to provide a confidence rating of their
opinion. Once again, subjects in a hindsight group estimated
the likelihood of the 'actual' outcome to be higher than did a
control group, despite the fact that some were told that one
outcome occurred, and the others were told that the *other*

outcome occurred! In other words, whichever outcome occurred, subjects found the results unsurprising. Hindsight leads people to believe that they know more than they do, that events which occur were more obviously likely to occur than they were, and generally gives an illusion of understanding where it is clearly not warranted. The implications of this are profound. People believe that events are more predictable than they are, and therefore have 'grounds' for supposing that other people should have been able to foresee outcomes better than they could have done.

The problem is that after the fact, it is always easy to find reasons why what happened did indeed happen, while at the same time ignoring all the other facts which, had things been different, would have explained any other outcome just as well. Scientists with theories about data, historians 'explaining' the causes of historical events, and the layman 'explaining' the social and political world about him are all in the same position. It is easy to concentrate on those facts which fit the outcome, and so feel that one understands and has the explanation for things.[25] At a far more trivial level, those of us who have watched people playing fruit machines will most likely have encountered the rather strange intuitive 'understanding' which players can have. If nobody has won for a while, players reason either that the machine is having a 'no-pay' period or that it is about to have a 'payout'. Whatever the outcome, the prediction will be reinforced, so although the understanding has no predictive value, players may think that they are actually understanding something.

The human mind seems to be exceptionally well-tuned to making coherent and consistent models out of small numbers of facts and limited amounts of knowledge. Given a datum, hindsight seems to rely upon the ability to select from a mass of conditions those which are pertinent to the datum. These conditions are then the model within which the 'outcome' is explained. This surely is an important part of understanding, since understanding why an event took place relies upon isolating the factors which brought about the event. But this is not enough: it amounts to a mere extension of primary processing. Suppose that in some situation there were several possible outcomes, mutually exclusive but all roughly equally likely, and all dependent upon a large number of non-trivial factors. It does not increase our powers to predict what will happen in similar circumstances if we simply explain what did happen without explaining also why, on this occasion, the other possible outcomes didn't happen. I am not saying that people *never* do this, just that it is typical not to.

One rather profound limitation on our understanding derives from the very mechanics of primary processing. Suppose that you are affronted by outbreaks of violence at a number of recent heavy-metal rock concerts. You may be thinking that heavy-metal with its high noise levels and distorted sounds leads to violent feelings and acts. What constitutes evidence for this claim? You might argue, as would many, that the high violence levels at heavy-metal concerts is the evidence. Say that at ten heavy-metal concerts there was violence reported. Sounds convincing. 'But wait,' you say. 'What about the possibility of heavy-metal concerts where nothing was reported?' After a search through the entertainment columns of the papers (not the headlines!) you find that there were thirty concerts of this sort where nothing of the sort happened. 'So what?' says the local council leader. 'At 25 per cent of these concerts there is violence, so action must be taken.' At each of these levels of analysis, heavy-metal is going to be banned or heavily policed, perhaps leading to more violence through mutual suspicion. More to the point is the analysis of the incidence of violence in other settings, say concerts which are not in the heavy-metal genre. If there is violence there too, one would be less inclined to accept that heavy-metal led to violence.

In a full contingency table, there are, in fact, four cells, as depicted below:

	Heavy metal concert?	
	yes	no
Violence? yes	10	7
no	30	25

In normal life, people appear to concentrate first on the top left cell, presumably because this gives rise to the idea in the first place. They then concentrate on the bottom right cell, and only after that are they likely to concentrate on the others.[26] This amounts to following a strategy of trying to *find confirmation* for the theory. This is not restricted to my hypothetical example, it is a very general phenomenon called 'illusory correlation'. It may interest statistically naive readers that the above hypothetical example suggests no relationship of the sort being described. That is, the probability that violence is related to heavy-metal concerts is not acceptably different from chance.

If understanding proceeds by trying to fit data into an existing model, then there should be evidence of a 'confirmatory strategy' in a wide variety of settings. Indeed, there is such evidence, ranging from simple laboratory settings to complex real-life tasks. At the laboratory end of the continuum, consider the following task devised by Peter Wason.[27] I have a rule in mind which specifies the possible continuation of the following sequence of numbers: 2, 4, 6, ... Your task is to ask me questions to try to find out what the rule is, and when you think you know the rule, announce it and you will be told whether you are right or wrong. With this task, Wason found that most people thought of a possible rule (e.g. going up by 2s) and then 'tested' it by offering numbers consistent with the view (e.g. '8'). Given the reply 'yes' by the experimenter, this was taken to support the rule. But how informative is such a discovery? Not very, since it is also consistent with a large number of other possible rules, such as 'the series is an ascending set of even numbers', or 'the next number must be bigger' or 'the next number must be the same as the last one or bigger', and so on. The only way to narrow down on a *set* of possible rules is to rule out other possibilities by asking questions that lead to a possibility of rejecting the view in mind. Subjects tested by Wason showed an overwhelming tendency to adopt a confirmatory strategy, however, and his examples make fascinating reading. Such a strategy has also been observed in the more complex setting of discovering explanations in science.[28]

This catalogue of fallacies in reasoning is by no means exhaustive, and in technical settings great care is usually exercised in order to replace informal reasoning with the carefully studied and developed apparatus of probability theory, scientific control and statistical testing of hypotheses. These methods were not plucked out of mid-air, nor dreamt up by boffins who are scarcely human. Rather, they reflect a steady concern and hard work over the centuries by people who, while susceptible to the same fallacies of human reasoning as the next person, as a community gave us tools with which to reason that go beyond our individual capabilities.

As individuals forced to think heuristically, intuitively, and without a complete analysis of the facts, often in necessary ignorance of all of the facts, we are all prey to these and other limitations on our understanding. It is well worth entertaining the view that in situations that really matter, we might be over-confident in our understanding of things. It is also important to realise how many of our intuitions are 'confirmed' in a way that is quite independent of anything approaching rational understanding. In a masterly paper on the problems, Einhorn[29] considers the example of a waiter in a busy restaurant, who doesn't have time to give good service to all of the customers he has to serve. So he makes predictions about who is likely to give a tip. Good or mediocre service is then given on the basis of these predictions. If good service leads to big tips, then the waiter will have had his intuitions confirmed! But note that to test his intuitions, should it occur to him, he would have to give poor service to those he thinks likely to give good tips, and good service to those he thinks would give poor tips. This will be perceived as leading to at least a short-term potential drop in income, so it is unlikely to be carried out, and even the reason why will reinforce the waiter's feelings that his intuitions are consistent and reflect reality.

IN CONCLUSION

We began by asking what intuition was. Our intuitive grasp of things, like other forms of understanding, is dependent upon mapping a situation onto a model of some sort. If the fit is good, we have the impression of understanding without having done very much thinking—an intuitive understanding.

When such mappings are made easily and result in predictively useful explanations of things, we say our intuitions are good. However, the bulk of this chapter has been concerned with situations where heuristic thinking leads to fallacy. This is of the utmost importance, since a failure to highlight these failures would be to ignore a key aspect of human mentality, and that is its fallibility. In a world where consistency and certainty are highly prized, the problems of overconfidence and misguided pseudo-understanding must be taken seriously. Knowing that each and every one of us is subject to these biases because of the very mechanisms that enable us to understand properly, knowing ourselves must include being prepared to question our own confidence in things.

On the whole, our understanding and our actions are entirely sufficient to enable us to form complex, advanced societies and live in them, build computers and televisions, and visit the moon. Heuristic reasoning works sufficiently well for many purposes, and by interacting with other people, by carrying out careful studies of things, and by accumulating knowledge over the centuries, fallacies come out and can be avoided. It is not the message of this chapter that the human species cannot think and achieve. Rather, it is at the *individual* level that one must take care. An open mind is not falsely confident.

The impact of what we have been discussing is being felt in the 'real world'. Fallacious reasoning is at last being scientifically studied in clinical diagnosis, the interpretation of psychological screening tests, the understanding of risk and the financial aspects of risk, the selection of candidates for jobs, rules for the allocation of scarce resources, and many more. One looks forward to the day when an understanding of these things is as important a part of education as is learning to read and add up.

CHAPTER 5

Reasoning Logically

If off-the-cuff decisions may fail, and if our estimates in the face of high levels of uncertainty may fail, then there is always the saving grace that man is logical. Surely, one might argue, people know how to produce logical arguments, and they recognise the difference between a logical and an illogical argument. Or shall we once more find only evidence of human fallibility? The present chapter is a description of some aspects of human reasoning in situations where logic is the yardstick. As with other aspects of understanding, we shall relate the results of observing people's behaviour to the kind of processing supporting this performance. First let us examine terms such as 'logical' and 'logic'.

They are a common enough part of the thinking man's vocabulary, and clearly denote something which is desirable, by-and-large. In many people's minds these expressions are closely associated with words like 'reasonable', 'rational' and 'sensible'. However, the technical use of 'logical' should be carefully disentangled from these related expressions. To illustrate one distinction, consider the following chain of reasoning:

If a Martian lands, people panic.
A Martian has landed.
Therefore, people are in a panic.

From a logical point of view, there is nothing at all wrong with this. If one takes the *premises* (the first two lines) as true, then the conclusion is true. If someone uttered this in good faith, we might have reason to doubt their sanity, but as a self-contained statement, it is perfectly logical.

Now contrast the next example:
Women who are pregnant put on weight.
Mary is putting on weight.
Therefore Mary is pregnant.

Someone who utters this sort of thing might be speaking about sensible things, it may even be the case that both of the premises are true and also that 'Mary is pregnant'. But from a logical point of view, the conclusion simply does not follow from the premises. This is probably self-evident to most readers, but can be spelled out in the following way: Pregnancy is only one reason for putting on weight; perhaps Mary has been eating too much, or taking too little exercise, etc. In brief, while 'Mary is pregnant' is a *possible* conclusion, it is not a logically necessary one. For a conclusion to be logically valid, it must necessarily follow from the premises. So anyone arguing after the style of our second example is 'being illogical'.

It is a simple matter to draw up a table illustrating what type of conclusion follows from various combinations of premises. To do this, we shall use the following conventions. The first premise will be in the form IF p THEN q. That is, if some proposition p holds, then q follows. For the second line, we could state that p does indeed hold (p), or that it does not hold (not-p), or that q holds (q) or that q does not hold (not-q). This gives rise to four possible combinations of premises:

(a)	*(b)*	*(c)*	*(d)*
$p \rightarrow q$	$p \rightarrow q$	$p \rightarrow q$	$p \rightarrow q$
p	not-p	q	not-q
therefore q	no conclusion	no conclusion	therefore
			not-p

It is easy to check the conclusions here. With (a), we say that p brings about q, so if p then q follows. With (b), just because not-p holds, we cannot rule out the possibility that something other than p brings q about, making q a possible conclusion. We only know that not-p however, so the best we can say is that no necessary conclusion is possible. With (c), no conclusion is the best we can do again, since q could have been brought about by something other than p. With (d), we can conclude not-p, since not-q could not possibly occur if p occurred.

There is some evidence that people are not particularly good at applying these rules. For instance, in one recent study, Rips and Marcus[1] asked American college students to evaluate statements like:

If the ball rolls left, the lamp comes on.
The lamp comes on.
Therefore, the ball rolled left.

Students were allowed to conclude that this conclusion, and the others deriving from the table above, were 'never true', 'always true', or 'sometimes true'. With the present example, one cannot say that it is 'never true', because it is simply indeterminate. Nevertheless, some 16 per cent of responses were 'never true'. With statements of the type IF p THEN q, not-q, therefore not-p, the correct conclusion, 'always true', accounted for only 57 per cent of responses.

So although things are fairly simple up to now, it is apparent that some people do not give responses which accord with the principles of logic. There are several possible explanations of why these errors are made. Let us concentrate on one line of reasoning. Faced with a task of this sort, it is first of all necessary to appreciate that to be 'always true', the conclusion is logically necessary. Secondly, it is necessary to appreciate that IF p THEN q does not rule out the possibility of q following from other things, which might be characterised as IF {a or perhaps b or c or ...} THEN q, where a, b, c ... etc. are just other possibilities. People who think that IF p THEN q, and q leads to THEREFORE p are either not recognising possibilities b, c, d, etc. or are not using it to judge necessity. In fact, they are treating the situation as though the first line is IF AND ONLY IF p THEN q, which is very different, since this specifies that the rule necessarily and only relates p to q.

What might this mean in practice? Well, one possibility is that people do not recognise that there may be other alternatives in a situation. For instance, compare:

If people commit murder then they go to jail.
John goes to jail.

And:
>   If the ball rolls left then the light comes on.
>   The light comes on.

A person reading this will have to interpret it in some way. A primary process search with the first example will find a plenitude of information in the knowledge base. Amongst this will be readily accessible information to the effect that there are many, many reasons why someone might end up in jail. Murder is only one of them. So it is relatively easy to convince someone that the first combination of premises leads to 'no conclusion possible'. In the second example, an arbitrary and artificial world has been depicted. It seems much less likely that a subject confronted with this pair of premises will think of other things which might lead to the light coming on, since they would have a foundation in pure fantasy.

Such a line of reasoning about a naive person's approach to a logic puzzle like this implies that the ease with which people think of alternatives, probably spontaneously, should be a determinant of whether they produce answers which conform to the dictates of logic. An interesting study by Markovits[2] revealed that in a sample of post-secondary students, there was indeed a correspondence between subjects' performance in a task where alternative possibilities for an event had to be listed and their performance on logical reasoning tasks which were essentially similar to those discussed above.

While it is doubtful that the ability to spot alternatives guarantees perfect performance in these tasks, it is certainly a necessary condition. But there is another feature of these tasks which can lead to problems. In a highly artificial version of the task, it is commonplace to present what amounts to an imaginary world. If someone reads that IF fzz THEN dff, they are likely to take it that the writer wishes people to suppose a world in which there are fzz and dff, but nothing else (otherwise it would have been mentioned). In fact, in the context of *language understanding*, it would be breaking the implicit contract between speaker and listener to announce that someone made an error of reasoning because they did not think of other *hypothetical* things. Indeed, one can see in the following discourse the way in which it is natural when reading to accept an IF statement as though it were an IF AND ONLY IF statement:

- The Southern General Hospital is extremely large and well-equipped. It takes all the head injuries in the West of Scotland. Late last night, a small boy was admitted following a car accident in which his father was killed . . .

Of course it doesn't follow that the boy has a head injury, at least not logically. Yet, unless assumptions of this sort are made, text comprehension would soon grind to a halt. It is clearly necessary to distinguish between pragmatic inferences made while reading discourse and logical, deductively valid inferences made in more analytic reasoning. One source of difficulty for people solving logic problems might be the transfer of habitual pragmatic inference-making to the domain of evaluating logical necessity.

OTHER INTERACTIONS BETWEEN KNOWLEDGE AND BEING LOGICAL

The use of *p* and *q* earlier signifies an important fact. The rules of logic stand independent of content. Our observations on p and q hold regardless of what the content of propositions p and q might be. Yet what has been said up to now suggests that a person's ability to apply the logical principle depends rather critically upon content. There is more evidence to support this contention. One well-known example is manifest in the various forms of a task initially devised by Peter Wason.[3] The question he asked was whether or not people would make use of the principles of logic in evaluating an IF–THEN rule. Subjects are given a rule like the following, taken from a study by Johnson-Laird and his associates:[4]

IF a letter is sealed THEN it has a 5d stamp on it.

Subjects see four envelopes before them, in the following way:

No. 1 Stamp-side up, with a 5d stamp
No. 2 Stamp-side up, with a 4d stamp
No. 3 Flap-side up, sealed
No.4 Flap-side up, not sealed

The task is to evaluate the truth or falsity of the rule by turning over as few envelopes as are necessary (in the logical sense). Readers unfamiliar with the problem might like to try it with four envelopes to get a better impression of what it is like to be a subject in this task. In fact, the rule under test was at one time well known, reflecting a property of the two-tier postal system. One could send an unsealed letter at a cheap rate (4d), but for sealed letters, the price was higher (5d).

In this experiment, almost all subjects turned over no. 2 and no. 3, which is the correct thing to do. Why is this the correct pattern? Well, in order to test a rule it is necessary to examine conditions which might enable us to refute the rule. If there is a sealed envelope (condition 3) and it has only a 4d stamp on it, then the rule has been broken, and is therefore false. In the same way, if an envelope with a 4d stamp (condition 2) turns out to be sealed when it is turned over, then the rule has been broken. These two selections are thus tests of the rule. In contrast, there is nothing to be gained from selecting no. 1, since the rule does not say that a 5d stamp cannot be used for an unsealed letter. In the same way, there is no point in selecting no. 4, since a not-sealed envelope could have either a 4d or a 5d stamp on it, and fit the rule.

Subjects had little difficulty making appropriate selections with this version of Wason's task. People seem to make the 'logical' choice. But the *original* versions of the task did not produce such a healthy pattern of responses. It is not difficult to appreciate why: the original had four cards with letters and numbers printed on, after the following pattern:

card 1	card 2	card 3	card 4
A	D	4	7

The rule to be tested was:
- IF a card has a vowel on one side, THEN it has an even number on the other.

This rule is precisely the same kind as the postal example. But it is much more difficult for most people. Indeed, the predominant choice pattern is to check A and 4. Now while turning A is a good strategy because it offers a test, checking

4 is quite pointless because there could be a vowel or a consonant on the other side, and either of these is allowed by the rule. The critical test is to turn over 7, because if there is a vowel then the rule is blatantly false. Just why people do not follow the optimal pattern is a little unclear. One highly likely explanation is that people have a natural bias towards confirming rules rather than towards testing them.[5] We have already encountered something similar to this in the previous chapter.

Our main concern here is with the difference between the postal example and the abstract version. Why do people do well at one and badly at the other? Let us approach it by invoking primary processing. On being presented with a rule, the language processor will attempt to map the elements of the rule, or the rule itself, into a high-level knowledge structure. But what structure? In the case of the postal scenario, there will be a straightforward structure for the two-tier mail system. From the point of view of social rules and the consequences of transgressing them, the memory structure should have one simple piece of information in it: *Under no circumstances put a 4d stamp on a sealed letter, or the person at the other end will have to pay, etc.* So if a mapping is made between the rule and this knowledge, there is a ready-made prescription for a test, which is simply to see if anyone is breaking the important rule. So rather than using some formal logical rule, perhaps people are merely applying the sensible everyday rule, which produces performance that looks logical.

This explanation would be consistent with our argument that primary processing is used wherever possible. The alternative is that people may have difficulty with 'abstract' versions because they do not contain references to everyday, familiar things. This seems false, however, since an arbitrary but imaginable assertion like

IF I eat beef THEN I drink gin

yields performance as bad as the abstract version.[6] In contrast, a study with the non-arbitrary rule shown below yields the logical pattern of behaviour:

IF a person is drinking beer, THEN he is over 18.

This is perfectly understandable as the 'underage drinking

rule', common to many cultures. The rules are designed to prevent underage drinking of alcohol, and the critical part of it is that it is bad to drink when you are under a certain age. This is the bit which is socially important. So a mapping onto this rule will induce a person to apply the appropriate test, but not because of the logic of the problem. Indeed, the investigators of this version of the task[7] found that with a slight change to the rule, people performed badly again, verifying the rule rather than testing it:

IF a person is under 18, THEN he is drinking coke.

It appears that sometimes people seem to be logical in the selection task, and sometimes not. It all depends upon the content of the problem, and the effect of this in turn seems to depend upon what is found in long-term memory as a result of primary processing. It will be clear from this how difficult it is to uphold a view that people have a set of logical principles in their head which is called up and applied in the appropriate situation. Although some psychologists hold on to the view that there is such a thing as a mental logic, there is strong evidence that logical reasoning, like other sorts of reasoning, is not independent of content but that the very way reasoning is carried out is strongly dependent upon content.

In his excellent treatment of this subject, Johnson-Laird[8] puts forward a number of other arguments against what he calls 'the doctrine of mental logic', arguing that it is much more meaningful to ask how people carry out tasks of reasoning than to ask whether people are intrinsically logical. Once again, processing accounts are more promising than any other approach.

REASONING WITH QUANTIFIED STATEMENTS

Language abounds with expressions which denote proportions of things—words like many, most, all, some, few, etc. These we shall call quantity expressions.[9] In logic, the best understood expressions are very close relatives of the natural language expressions all, some, and no(ne). Historically, logicians since the time of Aristotle were concerned

with understanding the rules for drawing logically valid conclusions within the context of the three-term syllogism. Although the syllogism has now achieved the status of a logical
dinosaur, it is still of interest to the psychologist, because not
only is it well understood, but it is a form which is ideal for
looking at how people reason with quantified statements.

Three-term syllogisms have two premises, each of which
contains a quantified expression, and a conclusion. The
question is always which non-trivial conclusion follows from
the premises. The following is an example:

    All actors are showmen.

    All showmen are extroverts.

    Therefore, all actors are extroverts.

This conclusion is valid, because it follows necessarily
from the premises. All syllogisms have three terms—in the
present case actors, showmen and extroverts, and can be
combined in the classical way using some, all and no. Consider the following case:

    Some dancers are showmen.

    Some showmen are extroverts.

    Therefore, some dancers are extroverts.

This syllogism has an invalid conclusion, but despite its sim-
plicity to anyone who has thought about syllogisms, colleagues
in philosophy inform me that logically naive students will
still think it valid at first, and certainly I have met intelligent
people myself whose first reaction was that it is valid. First,
let us see why it is not valid, and then try to assess why some
people think that it is on first sight.

First, what does 'some' mean? In logic, it means 'at least
one'. In other words, more than none. In everyday life, it
could mean at least one too, but more typically brings to
mind an amount somewhat greater than 10 per cent and
somewhat less than 100 per cent. Now let us see how a
representation of 'Some dancers are showmen' might be put
together. Philip Johnson-Laird (see note 8) has devised a
convenient and interesting way of doing this, and I shall use
his representational scheme. What the diagram shows is a
bunch of As, *some* of which are connected to Bs. The connection denotes 'is a':

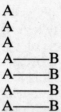

```
A
A
A
A———B
A———B
A———B
A———B
```

This depicts only part of the possible state of affairs which can be derived from 'some dancers (As) are showmen (Bs)', but it will serve for now. A similar diagram may be drawn for 'Some showmen (Bs) are extroverts (Cs)'. This is depicted on the left-hand side of the figure below. Then, by combining the two diagrams for the premises, a new figure can be produced, and this is shown on the right, below:

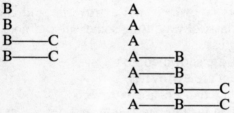

```
B               A
B               A
B———C           A
B———C           A———B
                A———B
                A———B———C
                A———B———C
```

From the combined diagram, it is clear that the conclusion 'some dancers (As) are extroverts (Bs)' follows from the premises. Johnson-Laird has suggested that when solving or evaluating syllogisms, people set up representations which are essentially like this in their minds—mental models of the situation—and it is to these that we should look if we are to understand how syllogistic reasoning takes place.[10]

Now, to return to the point that the syllogism is invalid. The representation of 'some' given above is not wrong, but it is incomplete. If some As are Bs, it is possible that there are some Bs that are not related to As. The same holds good for 'some Bs are Cs', of course. These possibilities are important for judging the validity of deductive inferences, because only necessary conclusions are considered valid. Thus, as Johnson-Laird suggests, a more appropriate representation of the two premises would be:

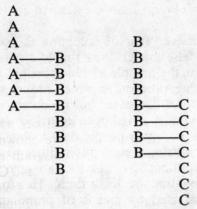

This new pair of representations can be combined in a variety of ways, two of which are depicted below:

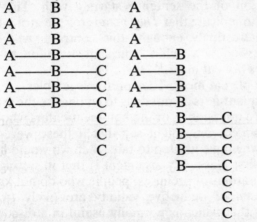

In the left-hand combination, it can be seen that at least one A is a B is a C, and so it corresponds to the conclusion. In contrast, the right-hand combination does not have one A that is a C, and so it is possible that there is a conclusion that 'No As are Cs'. Because of this possibility, it is not *necessary* that 'some As are Cs', and so to accept the premise as deductively valid would be an error. The principle is exactly the same as it was for the implication examples discussed earlier. Seek an alternative to the conclusion. If it is possible to find one which contradicts the conclusion, then the conclusion is not deductively valid. Such manipulations of models form the basis of Johnson-Laird's extensive account of syllogistic reasoning.

Let us return to the naive error of accepting the conclusion on the basis of a false model. Why should a person use an incomplete model in the first place? One possibility is a carry-over from applying procedures which are appropriate to the everyday use of language, but which are not sufficient for logic. When someone makes an assertion of the sort 'some people are Xs' or 'some people do X', they are normally trying to call the listener's attention either to the fact that not everybody is or does X, or else they are going to talk about the set of people that are Xs or do X. This focus of attention can be illustrated by means of pronominal anaphora, as discussed in Chapter 2:

Some people eat meat. They . . .

The continuation of the sentence starting with 'They' is almost certain to indicate that *They* stands for the group that eats meat. Interestingly enough, this contrasts with the quantity expression 'few' which can shift attention to the group that does *not* eat meat:[11]

Few people eat meat. They prefer vegetables.

What these quantifiers do not do is to emphasise the meat-eaters which are not people, or the non-meat-eaters who are not people. Indeed, one might say that if these were the groups about which we wanted to talk, then we would have said so in the first place. My argument is that in setting up initial representations of premises, people who do not know the requirements of deductive validity are likely to incorporate only that which is normally useful in a discourse context. What this means is that they may falsely accept a conclusion as valid because their initial models are not appropriate to the task at hand.

Of course, a little learning about reasoning over syllogisms and people quickly get away from this kind of error. If one were trying to defend the view that people are quite capable of using a set of context-independent rules of logic, then one might say that once it is made clear that the rules of logic must be used, people will use them, and will use a logical representation of quantified statements rather than the more restricted natural-language one. However, in terms of performance, even knowing what the rules are does not guarantee good performance. Here are the premises of a syllogism that is notoriously difficult:

Some boys are athletes.

No cowards are athletes.

It is advisable to try it, first in your head, and if this fails, resort to a pencil and paper. The problem is to establish any valid conclusion. As noted, Johnson-Laird argues that when confronted with a syllogistic reasoning task, people form representations (mental models) of the premises and attempt to combine the representations with a view to finding an internal representation which holds regardless of how the premises are combined. This can be taken as a valid conclusion, but only if all possible combinations have been checked, since even one failure to preserve the relationship is enough to signal the putative conclusion as invalid. And of course, some combinations of premises allow for more possible combinations in models than others. The example given above requires three alternative models to be formed, before the correct valid deduction can be established (some of the boys are not cowards). Johnson-Laird puts forward a very detailed process model for model construction and manipulation which is capable of correctly solving all possible syllogisms of this sort. He ascribes the difficulties which people have to the way information is represented in short-term working memory, and to consequent failures to evaluate all possible models.

THE CONTENT OF SYLLOGISMS

With the implication problems, there was ample evidence that reasoning was influenced by the content of a puzzle and was not just a function of its logical-abstract form. As with implication, so it is with syllogisms. Research on the conflict between attitudes and logical reasoning was well underway by 1928.[12] But more recent research is better controlled and of correspondingly greater value. There can be a basic conflict between the pragmatic plausibility of a deduction and its logical validity. For example, the following syllogism has a

valid conclusion, but one which is pragmatically unacceptable. As a statement in relation to the world, it is simply
implausible:

Some of the weightlifters are jockeys.
All of the jockeys are weaklings.
Therefore some of the weightlifters are weaklings.

There is evidence that if a conclusion is in conflict with
truth in the world, then people have a resistance to accepting
the conclusion even if it is valid within the confines of the
logic task in which it is presented. Evans and his colleagues[13]
presented a number of difficult three-term syllogisms which
had conclusions that were either pragmatically acceptable or
not. For instance, the following is one of their believable
conclusions:

Some highly trained dogs are not police dogs.
while the following is an unbelievable conclusion.

Some millionaires are not rich people.

The materials were arranged so that within the context of
a logical reasoning task, the conclusions could be either valid
or not. The investigators found that subjects were more
inclined to accept pragmatically believable conclusions than
unbelievable ones. Furthermore, if a conclusion were in fact
invalid, and it were also unbelievable then it was more likely
to be rejected, and classed as invalid. Certainly then, it is the
case that the acceptance of logical validity is a function of
believability. Once again, primary processing—matching a
conclusion to knowledge of the world—is seen to influence
the outcome of logical reasoning.

Of course, this experiment, like others, can be interpreted
as only showing that people resist accepting conclusions they
know to be untrue, even if they are logically valid. In a more
recent study, Oakhill and Johnson-Laird [14] carried out a test
of the idea that beliefs can alter the course of reasoning at a
much earlier stage than is revealed by the Evans study. Their
method was to present pairs of premises and ask subjects to
draw a valid inference from the pair, if any. Some of the
premises were believable, and some of them were not. The
premises were sufficiently complex that considerable processing was required to solve the puzzles, and in some cases
no valid conclusion was possible. Oakhill and Johnson-Laird

argued that should there be any effects of believability, then these could result from processes of forming conclusions rather than from simply evaluating conclusions already given. They found that if premises lead to a valid conclusion, then people are more likely to respond with that conclusion if it is believable than if it is not believable. If the premises do not lead to a valid conclusion, then people are much less likely erroneously to state some conclusion as valid if the premises seem to be leading towards a conclusion which is not believable. Thus beliefs actually influence the spontaneous production of conclusions within reasoning tasks, and the effect is not simply restricted to evaluating the validity of conclusions presented by experimenters. Oakhill and Johnson-Laird suggest that once a pragmatically acceptable conclusion has been thought of, and is being tested for logical validity in the way discussed earlier, perhaps the search for alternative mappings between the mental representations of the premises is curtailed. In contrast, an unacceptable conclusion (like 'some of the millionaires are not rich people') would lead to a more sustained effort of testing to see whether it is, indeed, logically necessary. Certainly, this plausible account would produce the pattern of results which the investigators discovered.

Both of the studies described above, and others, show that there is a bias in people to search more for counterexamples if the conclusions do not make pragmatic 'sense' than if they do. Such a tendency means that the truth value of a conclusion with respect to the real world is taken by the processor as being so important that it overrides or controls the application of the procedures necessary to check what follows logically from what.

DO PEOPLE REASON LOGICALLY?

What we should be asking is not this question, but rather *how* people reason within the dictates of logic. The evidence reviewed above shows not only that people can reason within the dictates of the requirements of a logical test, but also that they frequently do not. But what does that little phrase 'reason within the dictates of logic' mean? Logic is the name of a discipline in philosophy, a discipline which is concerned with the kinds of conclusion that necessarily follow from a set of premises. It is a technical subject akin to mathematics. Indeed, Bertrand Russell claimed that logic was pure (as opposed to applied) mathematics.[15]. Since it is concerned with what necessarily follows from what, it clearly bears some sort of relationship to human reasoning, since people are certainly not always wrong about what follows from what. But the relationship is *not* an especially simple one. One might say that if people reach a conclusion, based on a set of premises, and that conclusion conforms to the logically valid conclusion, that they have reasoned logically. This is perhaps the way we would describe it in everyday life. But this is not sufficiently accurate from a psychological point of view. The question to be answered is one of *how* such reasoning takes place, that is, by what set of procedures operating on what sort of data. Johnson-Laird's account is capable of explaining both how logical conclusions may be arrived at, and how systematic errors arise. The need to understand logical reasoning within a processing framework is also made clear by the way in which success at deriving logically valid conclusions depends upon the content of the problem, amply illustrated above. Logical necessity does not depend upon content. IF p THEN q, not-q, therefore not-p, holds good whatever propositions p and q may be. Yet people do not seem to be able to think in these abstract, content-free terms too easily.

One might suppose that trained logicians think logically. It would indeed be unfortunate if they did not perform rather well at tasks of deriving logically necessary conclusions. Suppose that trained logicians are better at the implication tasks than are less formally trained people. What might this mean? Think about it in terms of primary processing. On spotting any conjecture of an IF–THEN type, the logician's processor would presumably recover something at least as sophisticated as the one described above linking IF–THEN with p, not-p, etc. So the logician would have mapped the specific statement onto an abstract long-term memory structure. From then on, he will be able to see whether or not a specific conclusion is valid. Can one then say that he has reasoned in a content-free way? Not really, because the memory structure he used was merely something which he learned, and can apply when asked to reason logically. Indeed, it is salutary to realise that some of these simple representations from logic are quite difficult for beginners to learn. In so far as logicians perform better at tasks evaluated against the rules of logic, it is because they have acquired special knowledge structures and special recipes to apply in the face of the problem. Logicians are thus experts in the application of logical rules, formulated through years of individual enquiry resting on centuries of intellectual enquiry.

There are more formidable arguments which are a profound embarrassment for the view that we apply abstract logical rules in reasoning, problems which have been raised and analysed at length by Johnson-Laird (see note 8). Rather than say that people do or do not reason logically, it is better to say that they can reason about logical problems, that they can reason about the nature of logic, but that they do this by means of setting up mental models of possible states of the world. By exhaustively testing these models they may be able to guarantee a solution which accords with the dictates of a formally defined system of logic. But by looking at things in this way, whether people appear to reach logical conclusions, or whether they fall short, can be described within a single processing framework.

At a less technical level, it is obvious that people often fall short of reasoning out a logical conclusion because they fail to test all alternatives, or fail to recognise that alternatives are possible. Some of this is due to limitations of being able to 'spot' all possible alternatives, and some of it is due to not realising that there are possible alternatives, perhaps because of the representations set up by casting premises in natural language. Furthermore, the persistence with which alternatives are checked is a function of believability. Finally, people can sometimes find a valid conclusion for reasons which depend upon how the content of the problem relates to the real world. With logical problems, one has to guard against the intrusion of primary processing which is a fundamental mechanism for understanding things.

CHAPTER 6

Social Attribution and Understanding

One of your friends is upset. Why? Your wife or husband goes into a shop and comes out empty-handed. Why? You see someone trip over someone else's feet on the dance floor. Why did that happen? These are just a handful of commonplace events for which we may choose, on occasion, to offer explanations. Sometimes the problems can be more serious: Why is it that sometimes you can't sleep at night? Why did a coach crash in which thirty people were killed happen, and who is responsible? Why did a child in the care of foster-parents sustain a non-accidental injury when the local social work department knew that there were potential problems? Should someone lose their job as a result?

As soon as one attempts to answer these questions, great or small, one is providing reasons, or attributing causes, or attributing responsibility. If one had full knowledge of the circumstances and the backgrounds of the individuals concerned, one might suppose it possible to provide a logical analysis of the situation, and make one's attributions with confidence. However, things are seldom so easy: the investigations and decision-making processes of the law are notoriously complex. In the most serious instances, it is policy to accept that even in the face of 'all available evidence' it is better to rely upon the judgements of twelve independent jurors. Normally, of course, one has little chance of knowing 'all' of the facts anyway. The general question of how explanations are arrived at is one which has had a central place in social psychology since the publication of a seminal work in 1958 by Fritz Heider.[1] He claimed that the explanation of events and actions was a necessary (and commonplace) part of mental life because such explanations served to provide a means of predicting what would happen in similar circumstances. If in tutorials a teacher finds that a topic invokes reactions of dismay and disbelief often enough in enough students, then she will probably attribute the cause to the nature of the topic (or her treatment of it). If the same teacher finds that Freddy has difficulties with enough mathematical problems, but few others do, then she may well attribute the cause of this to Freddy's lack of mathematical ability or training. The actions to be taken are clearly different in these two cases.

Heider was primarily concerned with developing an account of the psychology of everyday life, and for him an appreciation of the causes of social events, and individual actions within a social setting was prime material. Since then, studies of the attribution of cause, responsibility and the like have become a major industry in social psychology. It is not the least surprising to find the literature on attribution theory packed with diverse types of studies using diverse situations, given the *a priori* magnitude of the topic. At one extreme, one find events depicted in simple written vignettes, with subjects being explicitly required to state the causes of the events so depicted. At another extreme, one finds experiments on subjects' *post-hoc* judgements of the influence that various protagonists in a conversation had on the others.

It is against this background of diversity that I shall attempt to pick out some of the landmarks of attribution studies.[2] Our aim, as before, is to pick out the characteristics of intuitive and 'reasoned' understanding, with one eye on information-processing explanations and the other on the limitations and biases of the understanding process.

EXPLANATIONS AS GAP-FILLERS

Everyday explanations revolve around chains of connected events, either real or imaginary, and occur either in response to a demand for an explanation, or because something is not

understood. What is the basis of something not being understood? A simple description might be couched in terms of
the primary process (knowledge-mapping) principle with
which we are now familiar: An event or a state is only
understood to the extent that it can be mapped onto an
existing knowledge structure.[3] To take a trivial example,
suppose that we are told 'The waiter at the restaurant spilled
soup over Mary's lap'. While the waiter and the soup are
mappable onto scriptal knowledge about restaurants, the
event is not. Because of the breakdown in primary processing, a new knowledge structure or set of structures will be
sought to enable a fuller understanding. In a real narrative
explanations are usually provided, since each event in a
narrative carries information relevant to the story-line. But
if no explanation is given, as is sometimes the case in real
life, then one is left to provide one's own explanations.

What is notable about this is that the kind of explanation
given or assumed will be a function for what or whom it is
being provided. For instance, a neurologist might suppose
that the waiter suffered from a clumsiness syndrome (no
fault of the waiter), a head waiter might explain it as 'in-
sufficient attention to the job' (the waiter's lack of responsibility), and the waiter's psychiatrist might see the explanation as the waiter's distracted state of mind because his
wife had left him. It all depends on how much we know, and
which knowledge structures are found during primary processing.[4]

Now consider a second case. You see a car career off the
road and crash into a lamp-post. How is this 'not understood'? There are strict conventions governing the movements of cars on roads. The event cannot be completely
mapped onto a knowledge-base which represents these conventions, so primary processing fails. Explanations which
might fill the gap include driver performance, automobile
failure, or something unusual about the road conditions. In
accordance with earlier arguments, which of the explanations is given or thought of in the first instance should
depend upon the availability of the different knowledge
structures, which is a function of interest and attitude.

Of course, our explanations are not always off-the-cuff,

especially where attribution brings about serious consequences, as in a case where the consequences include legal
proceedings. Indeed, it is in the jurisprudential literature
where one finds some sound leaders as to how causal attributions might be arrived at in normal social reasoning.

When something happens, it is the case that many
necessary conditions must be met to bring it about. For the
case of a car skidding on ice and hitting a lamp-post, it is
necessary that there is a driver in the car, the car is moving at
a certain speed, that there is ice on the road, and so on. For
the event to take place at all, all of these and many other
conditions must be present. Yet not one of them is *sufficient*
in itself to bring about the event. The entire combination of
conditions is considered by some philosophers (e.g. John
Stuart Mill[5]) to be the true cause, 'philosophically speaking'.
However, for everyday purposes one would never list all of
these things as causes. Since all of the elements listed above
are likely to be present on a road in the middle of winter, all
of them are readily understood in terms of primary processing—they are part of background knowledge. How does
some feature come to be picked out as *the* cause?

In their explanation of causal judgements in legal settings,
Hart and Honoré[6] argue that what is sought is an *abnormal*
condition in the circumstances of the accident, defined
against some notion of normality. The following could be
considered as potential candidates:

- The driver was driving abnormally quickly.
- The driver was abnormal because he was drunk.
- The road was abnormal in that a shopkeeper had
  created a sheet of ice by throwing a bucket of water
  over it.

In the first two cases, the cause is the driver's actions. In the
third, it is the road surface, and by similar considerations of
what is abnormal, it comes to rest at the shopkeeper's door-
step. The argument is, then, that the necessary condition
which is dignified as *the* cause is that which is abnormal. This
point of view makes eminent sense psychologically, since we
may recognise 'abnormal' as being a significant deviation
from what is represented in our normative background
knowledge about situations and their social and physical

constraints. Indeed, this rather attractive link between primary processing and that which is dignified as cause has been the subject of an interesting recent study carried out by Hilton and Slugoski[7] which shall be described shortly. For everyday social behaviour, including many extreme formalisations of it, as in law, the level of explanation which we initially adopt is that which is socially relevant, and thus at the level of our background knowledge. So, for example, while there is some flexibility in the speed at which we can drive down a city road, there is not much of a range. This is because speed limits are set for public safety, of course. Thus, if someone drives too quickly, this is the matter for concern, and it is at this level that causal arguments will be made. It would not normally be relevant to say 'The driver has the accelerator pedal pressed down one centimetre too much', although, strictly speaking, this is a necessary condition in many cases. Rather, what is abnormal is decided relative to our use of the roads and this is simply the speed of the vehicle. In brief, the level at which explanations are given depends entirely upon the presupposed relevant background.

Quite recent work by Kahneman and Tversky[8] has a bearing on the issue of level of explanation and on the things which seem to require explanation. They were concerned with situations in which something has happened, like a person one knows being killed in a car crash. As is well known, a common reaction is to say, 'If only X, then this would not have happened'. The investigators presented two versions of a story to two groups of subjects. In the story a character left his office to drive home, but was killed when he attempted to go through amber lights, although he attempted to stop when he saw a truck charging into the intersection at top speed. It was later established that the boy driving the truck was under the influence of drugs. In one version of the story (called the 'time' version), he was asked by his wife to leave his office earlier than usual, which he did. He drove home via his regular route, rather than the shoreside route which he occasionally took. In the other version of the story, he left his office at the usual time, but chose to take the coast route because it was a nice day (called the 'route' version). Kahneman and Tversky invited subjects to make 'if only' speculations. As might be expected given the foregoing argument, the subjects tried to 'undo' the unusual events. The investigators found four main categories of things which subjects would have changed: Changing the route (in the abnormal route version), changing the time of departure (in the abnormal time version), crossing at the amber light, and not having the drugged boy driving.

Now as was pointed out before, there are any number of conditions which have to be present to bring about an event of this sort. For instance, if the unfortunate victim had arrived at the lights seconds sooner or later, this would not have happened. But no subject mentioned this. Similarly, an infinity of possibilities could have prevented the particular accident from taking place. For instance, in the time version, it could be argued that 'if only' the victim had taken an alternative route, this would not have happened. Yet this was a relatively rare suggestion in the time version. The results seemed simply to suggest that subjects were most likely to 'undo' the accident by suggesting that the abnormal condition be restored to a more normal value. Abnormality for them was entirely in terms of what was normal behaviour for the victim. In reality, of course, one truly surprising thing, that which could not be predicted, is that at that particular time that car and that truck would be at that particular location. This underestimation of the role of chance is a serious bias in human explanation in many areas, but derives rather directly from the machinery of social understanding.

Let us now turn to some of the rather more direct studies of attribution which have been carried out in psychology. They concern both the rationality of explanation and the biases which occur in the determination of causes.

CAUSALITY JUDGEMENTS WITH VIGNETTES

Consider the following simple event:
John kicks the dog.
Why did John do this? Quite plainly, as things stand, you

could not give even a quasi-logical explanation, although you could find some possible explanations. One might suppose that the event has something to do with John. Perhaps he hates dogs and is a cruel person. Such an explanation is in terms of John's *disposition*. Alternatively, there might be something special about the dog: it might be an habitually aggressive dog frequently growling at people. This explanation is in terms of the dog's characteristics, the *stimulus* towards which the *person* acted. Yet another possibility is that the action was due to a peculiar one-off event. Perhaps the dog, normally good-natured, was frightened because Fred accidentally trod on its tail. The dog barked at Fred who thought it would bite and kicked out in an out-of-character panic. The cause is mostly just the particular unusual circumstances. What is required is more information of various types if one is to give a reasoned judgement. One may well have particular attitudes towards things which puts one of these different loci of explanation into mind rather than the others, and such attitudes will be peculiar to the actual event itself. Yet given more information, one might try to make a logical attribution.

To decide amongst the person, the stimulus and the circumstances, at least the following additional information is what many attribution theorists consider to be vital.[9] I shall put it as a set of questions:

(a) Has Fred usually kicked this dog in the past? If the answer is *yes*, this shows high *actor consistency*.
(b) Do other people kick this particular dog? If the answer is *yes* this shows high *consensus* over actors in the face of the stimulus.
(c) Does Fred kick dogs in general? If the answer is *no* then this particular stimulus shows high *distinctiveness*.

It is obvious that answers to such questions serve to change the plausibility of explanations for the event. Consider the following case, in which there is high consensus, high consistency, and high distinctiveness:

Event:	John kicks a dog.
	Almost everyone else kicks this dog.
	(High consensus).
Background:	John hardly ever kicks any other dog.
	(High distinctiveness)
Information:	In the past, John has almost always
	kicked this dog. (High consistency).

Such information forces one to suppose that there is something odd about this dog. For instance,

It is an odd dog.

It's the kind of dog everyone has to kick.

It is probably an habitually aggressive dog.

might be some of the explanations.

To get the feel for these kinds of constraint, readers are advised to make up similar event–background vignettes for low consensus, low distinctiveness, high consistency (LLH), and LLL configurations, since these are the most straightforward. The following table shows the patterns of attribution of cause which were suggested for various patterns of evidence by Kelley[10] in his now classic treatment of attribution:

Consensus level	Consistency level	Distinctiveness level	Resulting locus of cause
low	high	low	actor
high	high	high	entity
low	low	—	circumstances

Kelley supposed that when presented with the appropriate 'baseline' information, people would use it in a rational manner to draw conclusions about cause and reason. In originally conceiving of this line of attack, Kelley based his ideas on a somewhat different philosophical tradition from that outlined above—that of Hume and Mill. The idea here is that to infer the cause of an event, one uses information about the *covariation* between events, that is, how often the covariation occurs. For example, if every time I get hungry my stomach rumbles, there is high covariation between the two. This would lead me to conclude that the cause of my stomach rumbling is lack of food, for instance. Kelley thought that people would normally seek covariation in ormation along the 'dimensions' of distinctiveness, consistency and consensus. Here, we have paid more attention to the abnormal conditions account, which derives from the more recent philosophical work of Mackie.[11]

It is important to realise that the three 'dimensions' under discussion can be interpreted in both philosophical frameworks.

If people are provided with the three sorts of information described above, then one might well expect them to make judgements in accordance with the pattern given in the table earlier, provided that there are no reasons to give differential weightings to the credibility of each of the pieces of evidence. A straightforward test of this was carried out in a well-known study by McArthur.[12] She presented a number of single sentences describing events together with consensus, distinctiveness and consistency information, such that each could occur at high, low or medium levels. Her results broadly conformed to the patterns predicted, and so they offer some support for the view that each of the sources of information is normally used and integrated.

There was one important caveat resulting from her experiment, however. Subjects seemed to be less influenced than they should be by *consensus* information. The implications of this are great: it means that one is inclined to miss, ignore or not use information about what *most* people do in response to similar situations. In fact, we have already encountered an example of a failure to use consensus information in the work of Kahneman and Tversky, and others (Chapter 4). In the present context, it indicates a tendency to pay more attention to the individuals in a set of circumstances than to the chances of the event being the rule.

These results are broadly consistent with the view that people make use of consistency and distinctiveness information, and to a lesser extent consensus information, a result replicated in a similar but improved experiment by Jos Jaspers and his colleagues.[13] But the question must be raised as to *how* this information comes to be used. Kelley believed that some analysis of covariation was used. Jaspers and his colleagues characterised the process as one of applying a set of content-free logical rules. Briefly, in this account consensus, distinctiveness and consistency information are supposedly coded to indicate whether or not the target event occurs in the presence or absence of each of these possible causes. Jaspers devised a formal set of inference rules which could then be used to allow attributions to be made on the basis of the particular information configurations which were possible. The assumption here, of course, is that people bring some mental equivalent of such a set of rules into play when making attributions. We shall not go into this model, since the knowledge-driven account of Hilton and Slugoski, to be discussed next, seems to fit the facts rather better. Instead, we shall simply note that the issue has some similarity to the 'mental logic' issue in logical reasoning.

ATTRIBUTION AND ABNORMAL CONDITIONS

Hilton and Slugoski (see note 7) have recently attempted to lay the foundations of a process model for attribution in the face of vignettes like those above. They suggest a knowledge-based approach based on the detection of abnormal conditions, which in many ways is an implementation of the principles of language understanding discussed earlier in this book.

First note that in order to understand a vignette at all, the initial stated event, action or whatever has to be interpreted against background knowledge. As has been argued at length, the processor should attempt to find a mapping onto structures in memory which are relevant to the event. The simplest case to take is some sort of event which can be mapped onto a memorial representation of what *normally happens* under a particular set of circumstances. Hilton and Slugoski give the example of script-based mappings, and compared the following pair of actions:

- Sally bought something on her visit to the supermarket.
- Sally bought nothing on her visit to the supermarket.

Suppose that these actions are interpreted with reference to a 'supermarket script' which represented what usually happens at a supermarket. The first example fits precisely with the script, since it is what people do at supermarkets. As a statement, it is simply not informative. The second example does not fit exactly, because the action is *abnormal* with respect to the supermarket script. It is informative.

The first point, a simple one, is thus that not all 'events', in isolation, stand in need of explanation. The second point is that, depending upon the presupposed background knowledge to which an event is related, distinctiveness, consistency and consensus will be differentially informative. Consider a high consensus case:

- Sally buys something on her visit to the supermarket.
- Almost everyone else buys something on their visits to this supermarket.

The high consensus statement is not at all informative. It contrasts neither with what happens normally at supermarkets, nor with Sally's behaviour which is equally normal. The same argument applies to low distinctiveness. However, *low* consistency information is informative.

- Sally bought something on her visit to the supermarket.
- In the past, Sally has hardly ever bought something on her visit to this supermarket.

Using script-based understanding, someone encountering 'Sally bought something on her visit to the supermarket' would have (as part of their model) the presuppositions 'Almost everyone else buys something on their visit to this supermarket', 'Sally buys something in almost every other supermarket she visits' and 'In the past, Sally has almost always bought something on her visits to this supermarket'. So telling people that this is the case should be perceived as uninformative. In contrast, given the event 'Sally buys nothing on her visit to the supermarket', each of these three things would be informative, since they could (potentially) be used as an explanation of the initial script deviation. A script can thus be thought of as being a stereotypical high consensus, low distinctiveness, high consistency data-structure.

Hilton and Slugoski consider scriptal statements, script deviations and others (e.g. 'Sue is afraid of the dog'), and examine the patterns of informativeness of the various possible configurations of covariation information, given presupposed 'norms' of behaviour. They predicted that subjects would be able to rate the informativeness of each of these sources of information in a way which matched the theoretical expectation. This prediction is not made by the theories of Kelley and Jaspers. The results of an experiment using a range of events and information configurations supported their model. In a further experiment they showed that the patterns of attributions which people make also conformed well with the theory.

The work of Hilton and Slugoski can be considered a step in the direction of working out a process-model of how attributions are made. One of the dominant features of their argument is that the informativeness of information depends critically upon evaluating against some presupposed background of what is normal. This may sound unsurprising, despite the fact that this has been one of the essential features of understanding which has been laboured throughout this book. Yet the covariation model, which ascribes the attribution of causality to the co-occurrence of events and apparently to nothing else, has been a dominant account of human attribution. For instance, on the covariation model, the important thing is the frequency with which things co-occur, and not whether high or low co-occurrence is abnormal. Hilton and Slugoski's account derives from a very different background, in which ordinary causal induction is assumed to proceed through counterfactual reasoning, and the determination of abnormal conditions.[14].

ATTRIBUTION BEYOND VIGNETTES: FUNDAMENTAL BIASES

The literature discussed above concerns 'ideal' situations in which the three types of information which attribution theorists have thought important in effectively determining cause have all been presented along with the event. The tasks used amount to explicit tasks of reasoning, in which subjects are expected to reason out likely causes in a systematic way. In real life one seldom has all of the information available, and one is seldom set the task of providing attributions before seeing an event. When one does give an explanation, it is not for the purposes of an experiment, but it is for social purposes or for one's own sake. Indeed, the bulk of attribution research has been concerned with situations where knowledge, of necessity, is extremely incomplete. Quite often, these studies are not of explanation *per se*, although they are closely related to it in that they have implications for the balance with which people or circumstances are seen as being generators of the locus of causes.

Although people's behaviour stems from an obviously complex interplay of situational and personal factors, there is evidence that people are biased in their perceptions of the relative importance of these factors. The earliest reported of these biases, now termed the *fundamental attribution error*, was noted by Fritz Heider in his seminal work. This error is a bias towards attributing another person's behaviour to his or her own dispositional qualities rather than to the circumstances in which the behaviour happened. The literature confronts one with a formidable array of evidence offering apparently strong support for this bias (see Ross [15]). Let us take one illustrative study as an example. Ross and his colleagues [16] recruited subjects for a quiz game involving tests of general knowledge. The subjects were randomly allocated to the roles of questioner, contestant or observer ('audience'), and saw the allocation happen on a random basis. The questioners made up their questions from their own general knowledge, and the contestants tried to answer the questions in a quiz setting at a later point.

After the quiz was over, questioners, contestants and observers alike rated the questioners and contestants on a set of judgements of competence. All parties (including the contestants) rated the contestants as having lower competence in general than the questioners. This *in spite of the fact that all the parties knew that the group to which they had been allocated was random*. Now it is quite clear that questioners were at an advantage because they could use their *own* specific knowledge to form the questions, while the contestants could and did face questions on anything. Yet this situational constraint was not given the value it should have been, because this should have led to approximately equal ratings of the two participant groups by all concerned.

A closely related bias can be illustrated by the following: Imagine a domestic scene in which husband and wife are sitting by the fire. They decide that they would like to go out to see a film, and the following conversation ensues:

> *Wife*: Did you get to the bank at lunchtime?
> *Husband*: No, 'fraid not. I was really busy at the office.
> *Wife*: I don't have any money. I wish you'd been to the bank.
> *Husband*: As I said, I was very busy.
> *Wife*: I don't suppose you 'phoned aunt Mary about Saturday either . . .
> *Husband*: Look, I've been so busy . . .
> *Wife*: You always leave the domestic details to me. You should do your share . . . etc.

This little scene may be extreme, though I doubt it. Regardless of imaginable facts, one can perceive two kinds of attribution going on here. The husband is explaining his behaviour in terms of external constraints—being busy and the like. The wife is explaining his behaviour in terms of a character trait—he (presumably habitually) 'avoids' chores through choice. She makes it sound like part of his personality.

The example should not be construed as a sexist attempt to illustrate some sort of nagging wife syndrome: it is an easy matter to reverse the husband/wife roles and leave the result just as recognisable. The point of the example is to illustrate an observation made many times within attribution studies: as observers, people tend to attribute the behaviour of others to the character or 'disposition' of the other; in contrast, in explaining or justifying their own behaviour (i.e. the 'actors'), people tend to attribute their behaviour to forces of circumstance. Of course, the example given above is an invented anecdote, but a large number of studies support the general claim. For example, Nisbett and his colleagues[17] asked a number of American male college students to explain in a paragraph their reasons for choosing their main university subject areas, and for liking their particular girlfriends. When writing about themselves, the students tended to write equally about their own qualities and attributes and those of their subjects or girlfriends. In contrast, when asked to write about their best friend's choices, they tended to emphasise only their best friend's characteristics, and not to discuss the subjects' or the girlfriend's characteristics. Thus there is a strong tendency to explain the behaviour of others in terms of their personal characters, but to explain one's own behaviour in terms of the circumstances.

Quite clearly, such an imbalance in the explanations of one's own behaviour and the behaviour of others is either inconsistent, or incomplete, or both. It is a bias in the way we look at the world, and leads to the corollary that we think of others as being more stable across situations than we think of ourselves as being. Indeed, this proposition can be tested quite readily. Trait descriptions, like 'aggressive', 'thoughtful', 'ambitious', 'friendly', and so on abound in all human languages, and people can be rated with respect to such traits, say on a five-point scale from *definitely describes*, through *sometimes describes*, *sometimes not* to *definitely does not describe*. Furthermore, one can rate oneself in this way, as well as others. The interest lies not in traits themselves, but in how extremely one would rate oneself and, say, a friend over a selection of trait questions. It can quite easily be demonstrated that one rates others as more extreme than oneself—that is, traits are more often seen as definitely describing or definitely not describing others more often than they are oneself (cf. Jones and Nisbett[18]).

Of course, the actor–observer differences in attribution represent only a tendency, albeit an important one, and there are a number of limitations on the generalisations made above. For example, the effect is weakened when the event being explained produces a negative or positive outcome. Thus positively valued outcomes, such as performing an act which is agreeable or pleasant, tend to be attributed to stable characteristics (such as 'being a nice person'). In contrast, events with negatively-valued outcomes tend to be attributed to situational factors. This finding holds up whether one is explaining the behaviour of others, or explaining one's own behaviour, although the trend is strongest for oneself.[19]

PROCESSING EXPLANATIONS OF ATTRIBUTION BIASES

It will be clear even from the small sample of studies described in the preceding section that we have strayed far from the relatively controllable situations discussed in previous chapters. Indeed, a broader survey of the voluminous literature in this field provides a multiplicity of caveats, exceptions and difficulties of interpretation which put any generalisations on a tenuous footing. Yet the fundamental attribution bias, the actor–observer difference, and the neglect of base-rate (or consensus) information remain as phenomena which occur in a wide range of settings. Whether each type of bias has a common explanation, or whether different processes lead to the same type of bias is difficult to ascertain, however. Until relatively recently, there has been a tendency to view social judgements as being sometimes rational, with error creeping in due to lack of information or because of distortion due to irrational motives and needs. Latterly, some theorists have begun to explore the possibility that heuristic reasoning, like that discussed in Chapter 4, might underlie the observed patterns of judgement and attribution. For instance, availability has been recruited as a possible source of bias.

The availability of information could perhaps explain the actor–observer differences in some instances. Thus it might be and has been argued that we know more of the circumstances under which we ourselves act than we know of those under which others act, and thus the potential explanatory field is more restricted when giving attributions about others.[20]. Such an explanation relies upon the idea that there are naturally occurring biases in the type and richness of information available depending upon whether one is actor or observer. A closely related argument is that aspects of the environment, including actors, which are prominent for some reason may capture our attention, and thus provide a starting point for attribution processes. The impact of increasing perceptual availability in various ways has been investigated in a number of very interesting but simple studies. Thus, in one study, it was demonstrated that the influence of a trivially highlighted member of a discussion group as being greater than that of others. Thus the same black man was rated as having a stronger influence on a group composed of five whites and himself than on a group composed of three blacks and three whites, although the behaviour of the group was constant over the two conditions. Similar results have been found for sex (e.g. one outnumbered woman versus an equal balance in a group), and even for illumination. If a member of a group is prominently lit, then his influence is rated higher. [21] These observations show some of the intriguing variables which have a measure of control over the loci which might serve as a base for making attributions. Furthermore, just as the salience of another can be manipulated, so too can the relative salience of aspects of oneself. Thus Duval and Wicklund [22] showed that when actors could see themselves in a mirror, or even when there was video-recording equipment in the room, they attributed their own behaviour more to themselves than they did in the absence of such equipment. These are situations which make actors more self-conscious, and perhaps the new attribution pattern is the result of the actor seeing himself as others would normally.

The interpretation of the results of experiments on complex social judgements are certainly worth considering from this point of view, and the potential importance of availability has received considerable attention, as have other heuristic-based theoretical ideas. [23]. There is at least a possibility that the complexities of biases in social judgement may one day be understood in relation to the mechanisms of understanding being unravelled by cognitive scientists. Indeed, an effort in this direction is desirable from both perspectives.

We have enquired as to whether socially significant biases are explicable in terms of the machinery of understanding as conceived of by cognitive psychologists. For instance, use of the availability heuristic might explain certain socially significant biases. But one should also appreciate that *what* we try to understand and the models with which we think about things are, in large measure, in the service of social interaction. The social evolution of patterns of thinking has to be appreciated by those who study cognition, just as the ubiquitous constraints on how we think must be recognised by social psychologists. This is an old dialectic, but that does not mean that it is not significant.

CHAPTER 7

Understanding Understanding

Our tour of various aspects of human understanding has been limited in two rather different ways. First, the perspective taken has been almost entirely bounded by experimental psychology and cognitive science. Secondly, only a sample of the work in these disciplines has been reported, though it is hoped that sufficient has been presented to act as an appetiser. In this final chapter, I shall attempt to evaluate some of the theoretical and practical aspects of the scientific study of understanding as portrayed within our somewhat limited frame of reference.

What is the Value of Studying Understanding?

One might approach this question from both practical and theoretical perspectives. Let us begin with the purely practical. Some of the results of studies of decision-making under uncertainty have found application in a number of areas, in business, clinical and administrative settings. This constitutes the commonplace flow of information from research to application. It is fair to say, however, that this is largely restricted to fields where there is a recognised need for established procedures, and while laudable, it is not the most interesting application. What is striking is the pressing need to replace intuitive judgement with the careful and scientific analysis of new types of decisions as they arise, and sometimes this will be difficult to recognise. Perhaps a solution to this rests in general education, a point to which we shall return.

A demand for the scientific analysis of understanding in a practical setting has arisen through the effort to apply new technology on a broad scale. One major example revolves around the development of expert systems. An expert system is a bunch of related computer programs that enables the user to get assistance in solving some problem. Such things are obviously highly desirable for the general public as well as for industry and other corporate settings. A tax advice system, for example, would be extremely useful for many people. In these days of overloaded teachers, tutorial programs in schools and universities would be of very great value. Such programs are known as 'expert systems' because they purport to embody the expertise of human experts in the field in question. This expertise is not merely a set of facts, but is a complete set of skills, including knowledge of what questions to ask a user in order to give advice, and problem-solving methods to apply in solving difficulties.

What this means is that the program of an expert system must be designed to reflect the way an expert understands the problems of his clients. In turn, this means that some way must be found to discover just what this understanding is. As the reader will probably appreciate, while an expert may be able to verbalise some of the rules and tricks which he uses, there will be much that cannot be elicited in this way. Understanding does not come in cans which can be opened on request. Understanding how an expert understands is one of the most interesting challenges currently facing the cognitive scientist who is interested in understanding itself.

From a computer scientist's point of view, a good technique would be one in which a computer program asked an expert a series of questions, and from the replies deduced the data and the strategies used by the expert. This method, which we might call automatic knowledge acquisition, has an obvious appeal, and systems of this type are being experimented with.[1] But notice that the program itself must model understanding in some sense in order to be able to ask appropriate questions and then model the expert. This is so difficult that it is a genuine cognitive science problem, the attempt to develop such systems being itself an aspect of the study of understanding.

Another technique is for an expert in a certain field to work with a cognitive scientist who uses the whole armoury of cognitive science to try to formulate the expert's understanding. This strategy is giving rise to a new breed of experts on knowledge elicitation called 'knowledge engineers'. Because of the inchoate nature of studies of understanding, working with an expert in an area is as much an act of research as it is a simple application of what we know about cognition already.

Another new term which has appeared in recent years is 'cognitive ergonomics', the term ergonomics meaning the study of efficient work methods. In cognitive ergonomics, emphasis is placed on how users of various facilities understand the facilities they are using. This work is not restricted in any way to new technology like computer systems, but that is where the primary applications have been. More and more people are in the position of having to use computer programs, from the increasingly commonplace word processor, through accessing information on office databases, to general-purpose systems like Prestel. Ideally, there should be no need for people to have to learn complex new instructions to be able to use such facilities, particularly since new versions of various systems appear at an alarming rate. The ergonomic problem is thus to:

(a) Make new things which have to be learned as easy as possible for us to learn, and to prevent misconceptions which might lead to serious error or misunderstanding of what the system is doing.

(b) Make the means of 'talking' to the system as easy as possible. This really means making the system capable of understanding expressions in terms as near to natural language as possible, in many cases, and giving the program facilities to check that the user knows what he or she is doing.

Let us consider the second point with the aid of a simple example. Suppose that you are using a database system that has information about the marks which all students got on all courses in every year at an educational establishment. You might put in a query like:

'How many students got more than 40 per cent in the formal semantics exam in 1958?'

The answer comes back 'NIL'. What does this mean? Well, because of the normal machinery of human understanding, most people would fairly take it to mean that 1958 was a bad year for formal semantics! But suppose that all the computer system had done was find that there was no formal semantics class in 1958. This would give a nil return all right, but from a user's point of view, an informative answer would have been:

'I don't know of any formal semantics class in 1958.'

Fitting the program output to the expectations of people would obviously overcome this, and such a program exists.[2] But the solution to this problem relies upon the analyses of what assumptions people make in normal dialogue regarding informativeness and other aspects of the implicit contract, outlined in Chapter 2.

The idea of a general-purpose natural language interface is immeasurably more complex than this simple example, but even limited natural language interfaces are both useful and provide a continued stimulus for research into natural language understanding and production in humans.

These few examples serve to show how theoretical research and practical application are closely intertwined and well-motivated. There is a continued need for pure research, however. Just because there is an obvious way of applying a field of research does not mean that all (or even most) of the problems in that field have been solved. But theory benefits from practical matters, as it always has. By working with experts, new insights are being made into just what are the characteristics of expert understanding. This has potentially profound implications for education.

In a given subject area, education can be thought of as giving expertise to a novice. How does one achieve this end? The overall answer is to tell the novice the facts (shades of Dicken's Gradgrind) and to give problems to be solved or essays to be written so as to provide a sort of 'hands on' experience. At the next level down, the question arises as to how to implement such a process in a humane, sensible and effective way. It is important to realise that novices, be they children or adults, are not empty vessels waiting to be filled (Lakoff and Johnson call this the *mind is a container* metaphor). Novices already have knowledge which will predispose them to think of things in certain ways, including brand new material. In other words, they will have intuitions. When a new fact does not fit an intuition, a bold child may say that they do not understand that fact, and perhaps even why they do not understand it. A timid child may just think to herself that she does not understand and if she learns the fact at all, she will learn it parrot fashion.

Recent work has been aimed at the differences between novice and expert understanding, and is of great potential value in education. Consider novice (lay) intuitions about theoretical mechanics in physics. [3] This is a notorious area for 'invalid' intuitions. What happens to a ball when it is thrown off a cliff? The typical naive answer is that it travels straight out from the cliff, following the direction in which it was thrown. Then 'gravity takes over' and the ball starts to fall, ending up falling vertically. If asked why, one gets answers like, 'Well, to start with, the ball has force/impetus/ energy in it which dissipates over time, and then gravity takes over'. In terms of the facts, this is wrong. According to the valid laws of classical physics, (a) once motion has been imparted to the ball by a force, it will continue to move in a straight line in the same direction until it is acted upon by a new force, and (b) the force of gravity acts *constantly* on the ball.

Thus the ball's trajectory turns out never to be straight, but a curve which accelerates more and more toward the vertical.

What is especially interesting is that there is nothing silly about these false intuitive explanations. In fact, they are very similar to the kinds of explanation which were commonplace in pre-classical mechanics. [4] Early treatises on the trajectories of cannonballs, for example, used such explanatory schemes which go back at least as far as Aristotle. From a theoretical point of view, a particularly interesting common feature of many naive explanations about such mechanical phenomena is that they attribute much of the cause of paths to something like 'substances' put into objects. Thus 'force' is 'put into the ball' and 'dissipates with time'. Investigators in this area are examining the possibility that eliciting novice explanations will tell us something about the fundamental, intuitive ways in which people think about the familiar physical world.[5]

From a practical point of view, it seems to me that a thorough understanding of novice intuitions in all fields of learning is an important part of developing a more effective and humane system of education. If student and teacher alike could understand why and in what way intuition clashes with the more veridical models used by experts, then a feeling of natural understanding would replace feelings of inherent stupidity. While there is a clear place for accepting some things 'on trust' in a learning situation, it is important to get the balance right. While most good teachers have probably recognised these things for a very long time, the growing body of work on naive intuition will hopefully provide a more solid framework for continued improvement in educational methods.

There should be no reason to have to justify the scientific study of man's behaviour and understanding. I certainly hope that the chapters of this book make it clear that such scientific exploration is entirely possible. Doubtless there will be many readers who see that understanding must be much more complex than is being portrayed here. That is quite right. But it is a view that is different from one which rests on the assumption that one can never know how people understand, or what it is that makes them behave the way they do in certain circumstances.

This book began with a statement to the effect that with a little effort, one can easily understand the workings of an everyday mechanical device, because such things are substantial, and clear chains of causation can be seen in their workings. Process models in psychology make it just as easy to think about the workings of the mind. But the mind looked at in this way is the most complex information-processing system which we can imagine. I believe that the proper appreciation of this fact has been made possible through the emergence of cognitive science, and that we are currently witnessing the foundations of a theory of types of intelligence, with human intelligence as one of the types. The popular classification of intelligence is in terms of 'high' and 'low'. This common default metaphor, with its none too pleasant entailments, is long overdue for replacement.

The whole of this book is cast in terms of empirical psychology and cognitive science. Surely this misses the point of other types of understanding. Are there not parts of understanding which will not be accessible through such means? For example, appreciating poetry, paintings, sculpture, understanding emotions? Are these not truly intuitive things which are beyond the pale of science? I see nothing wrong with exploring what it is that people feel and think about such things, and what it is that brings about the impressions they have. These things are as much a part of life as the activity which we routinely call cognitive. Indeed, if we wish to get a full picture of human understanding it is essential to do this. But we shall not do it by intuition alone, if by intuition at all. We shall do it by reasoned scientific enquiry.

IN CONCLUSION: UNDERSTANDING PEOPLE

Most of our discussion of understanding and folly in reasoning has been cast in terms of the general framework of information-processing theory. It sounds a bit cold to many people to talk about the human mind in this way. It is also construed by some as offensive to have rationality, logic and even intuition replaced by constrained forms of information-processing. Sometimes we want to think of human beings as rational and logical, after all.

The assault on the perfection of human reason is not at all new, of course. It dates from classical times, and runs through the writings of almost all philosophers. In the work of Francis Bacon, for instance, one even finds prescriptive dictates about what to avoid in reasoning. More recently, the truly excellent book *Straight and Crooked Thinking* by the psychologist Robert Thouless[6] has pointed out in a popular way some of the fallacies of reason and traps in interpretation which lie in wait for the unwary. The present book serves in part to point out such fallacies once more. But it is about more than that. What I have tried to do is to indicate that many of these fallacies and biases are not reprehensible slips of reason, but are an intrinsic outcome of the sort of machinery which supports human understanding. It is unlikely that the biases and errors can ever be 'drilled out' of us by some sort of moral training programme; all we can do is increase our awareness of them.

If one wishes to find moral implications, I believe that they are there, however. Misunderstandings may happen, but they can be understood. Sometimes a person may deliberately mislead another, but we have little to say about that here. More often, misunderstandings arise because two people have different sets of assumptions which they bring to bear on a situation. If this turns out to be serious, it is important to try to bring this out, and not dismiss the other as simply bloody-minded. It is important to be able to see when this is happening to other people. We all know this of course, but we do not systematically educate ourselves or our children in these matters, and we could.

If we all had all the time in the world, and were well educated in logic, probability and decision-making, perhaps our intuitions regarding our own confidence in the choices we make and the advice we give would be realistic. But we don't have all that much time to devote to every one of the situations that we 'understand' and 'explain', even if we could all be educated in logic, and so on. Consequently, much of our thinking takes short cuts and is based on in-adequate information inadequately evaluated. Given what I think is the inevitability of this fact, there is a moral obliga-tion on us to question our certainty about things, particularly where other people are involved.

If the ideas about mapping and a feeling of intuitive 'knowing' are correct, then there is another potential trap which seems to me more readily avoidable. Rather than accept a feeling of knowing as meaning that one understands something, why not ask what the knowledge amounts to? People are so afraid of appearing ignorant that they will seldom do this, even to themselves. But to ask what one's understanding is, is to be in a position to replace 'certainty' with knowledge, and open the door to true and felt know-ledge rather than the mere nominal.

Chapter Notes And Sources

FOREWORD

1. A. Eddington, *The Nature of the Physical World* (London: Cambridge University Press, 1928); C.S. Sherrington, *Man on his Nature* (London: Cambridge University Press, 1940); K. Barth, *The Knowledge of God and the Service of God* (1937–38), delivered in the University of Aberdeen; G. Marcel, *The Mystery of Being* (1949–50), delivered in the University of Aberdeen.
2. A.J. Sanford, *Models, Mind and Man* (Glasgow: Pressgang, 1983).
3. B.E. Jones, *Earnest Enquirers after Truth* (London: George Allen and Unwin, 1970), provides a good history of the Gifford Lectures and the orientation of Lord Gifford himself.
4. J. Bronowski, *The Ascent of Man* (London: British Broadcasting Corporation, 1975).

CHAPTER 1

1. A. Eddington, *The Nature of the Physical World* (London: Cambridge University Press, 1928).
2. J.M.E. Hamilton and A.J. Sanford, 'The symbolic distance effect for alphabetic order judgements: A subjective report and reaction time analysis', *Quarterly Journal of Experimental Psychology*, *30* (1978), 33–43.
3. R.N. Shepard, 'Learning and recall as organisation and search', *Journal of Verbal Learning and Verbal Behavior*, *6* (1966), 156–63.
4. Because different laboratories used different standard descriptions the point was reached where there was disagreement about how introspection should be carried out. In retrospect, it is obvious that introspection is both more forthcoming and more homogeneous across subjects in some tasks than in others. The problem is thus to discover which tasks produce introspections and which tasks don't, and then develop a theory as to why. Perhaps the behaviourist

124

rejection of introspection was a necessary step towards thinking of introspection in these objective terms. Recently, there have been both conceptual and methodological refinements on this front: K.A. Ericsson and H.A. Simon, *Protocol Analysis: Verbal Reports as Data* (Cambridge, Mass: MIT Press, 1984).

5. The approach described here views the brain as a machine in which information is processed. For a detailed but significant theoretical paper, see A. Newell, 'Physical symbol systems', in D.A. Norman (ed.), *Perspectives on Cognitive Science* (Hillsdale, N.J.: Lawrence Erlbaum Associates, 1981).

6. Full process-models and associated experimental studies may be found in O. Svenson and K. Sjoberg, *Evolution of Cognitive Processes for Solving Simple Additions during the first Three School Years*, Cognition and Decision Research Unit report no. 1 (University of Stockholm, 1982). Earlier, but more accessible, is G.J. Groen and J.M. Parkman, 'A chronometric analysis of simple addition', *Psychological Review*, **79**, (1972), 329–43.

7. These generalisations permeate the literature, but an especially relevant discussion is given in J. Greenò, 'The structure of memory and the process of solving problems', in R.L. Solso (ed.), *Contemporary Issues in Cognitive Psychology: The Loyola Symposium* (Washington, D.C.: V.H. Winston and Sons, 1973).

8. D.E. Broadbent and M. Broadbent, 'Grouping strategies in short-term memory for alpha-numeric lists', *Bulletin of the British Psychological Society*, **26** (1973), 135.

9. The most extreme view is that everything which we learn, think anew, notice and decide takes place in the limited capacity system. Such a view attributes no mysterious processes to unattended operations going on in long-term memory. Although counter-intuitive, this view does explain why it takes as long as it does to become 'expert' at anything. For an interesting (but technical) discussion, see A. Newell and P.S. Rosenbloom, 'Mechanisms of skill acquisition and the law of practice', in J.R. Anderson (ed.), *Cognitive Skills and their Acquisition* (Hillsdale, N.J.: Lawrence Erlbaum Associates, 1981).

10. The discussion which follows is based partly on some principles discovered during the design of the first general-purpose problem-solving computer program. This is described in the classic book G.W. Ernst and A. Newell, *GPS: A case study in generality and problem-solving* (New York: Academic Press, 1969). Other more psychological discussions are given in the following, which was also used in the discussion here: A.L. Glass, K.J. Holyoak, and J.L. Santa, *Cognition* (Reading, Mass.: Addison-Wesley, 1979).

11. The interest is not just theoretical. One of the biggest problems with any kind of data storage is not just the storage itself, but the difficulty of finding just what is available when a particular thing is needed. Memory retrieval in computers is fast only when the data in memory are rigidly organised (by human criteria), and in no computational system does the amount of data remotely reach the amount stored in a

single human head. Indeed, considerations of how human memory works is now influencing how efficient, vast computer memories might be built. See, for example, G.E. Hinton and J.A. Anderson *Parallel Models of Associative Memory* (Hillsdale, N.J.: Lawrence Erlbaum Associates, 1981).

12. Strictly speaking, the rules governing the statement calculus.

13. D.A. Hinsley, J.R. Hayes, and H.A. Simon, 'From words to equations: meaning and representation in algebra word problems', in P.A. Carpenter and M.A. Just (eds), *Cognitive Processes in Comprehension* (Hillsdale, N.J.: Lawrence Erlbaum Associates, 1977).

14. See, however, Ericsson and Simon (note 4).

15. At one level, it is clear that this argument is not at all watertight. However, let us not forget that we are trying to understand how humans understand, and that of course includes how they understand understanding. For the time being, I am relying upon a certain amount of pragmatic acceptance on the part of the reader.

CHAPTER 2

1. See J. Lyons, *Introduction to Theoretical Linguistics* (Cambridge: Cambridge University Press, 1968).

2. Part of the historical background includes attempts to represent language within logical formulations, and part of it technological work on automatic translation (which is in fact closely related). More recently, continued impetus is coming from attempts to build 'natural language' interfaces to intelligent computer systems.

3. Identical arguments apply to the perception of speech sounds, of course.

4. A recent introductory book which has a good treatment of word-recognition problems is A. Garnham *Psycholinguistics: Central Topics* (London: Methuen, 1985).

5. This problem of so-called 'indirect speech acts' has been a puzzle long recognised by philosophers and linguists. The essential difficulty is that the surface form of utterances are often of a different type from their underlying 'intended form'. This raises problems for any theory which assumes that every utterance has something which is a 'literal meaning'. A philosophical classic in this area is J.R. Searle, 'A taxonomy of illocutionary acts', in K. Grunderson (ed.), *Minnesota Studies in the Philosophy of Language* (Minneapolis: University of Minnesota Press, 1975). See also J.L. Austin, *How to do Things with Words* (Oxford: Oxford University Press, 1962). For implications of these issues for the design of artificial (computational) language systems, see for instance, P.R. Cohen and C.R. Perrault 'Elements of a plan-based theory of speech acts', *Cognitive Science*, **3** (1979), 177–212.

6. The classic philosophical work on the contract-like nature of conversation: H.P. Grice, 'Logic and Conversation', in P. Cole and J.L.

Morgan (eds), *Syntax and Semantics. Vol. 3: Speech Acts* (New York: Seminar Press, 1975).

7. For a process-oriented description, see A.J. Sanford and S. Garrod, *Understanding Written Language* (Chichester: John Wiley and Sons, 1981). More details can be found in A.J. Sanford 'Aspects of pronoun interpretation: an evaluation of search formulations of inference', in G. Rickheit and H. Strohner (eds), *Inferences in Text Processing* (Amsterdam: North-Holland, 1985).

8. This argument is detailed in Sanford and Garrod (1981), quoted in note 7, above. Much of the discussion which follows is based upon the joint research introduced in *Understanding Written Language*.

9. A.J. Sanford, A. Lucas, E. MacDougall and J. Simons, 'Gender and number mismatches in the resolution of pronominal anaphora'. Unpublished research note, University of Glasgow Department of Psychology, 1985.

10. A. J. Sanford and S. Garrod, 'The role of background knowledge in pschological accounts of text comprehension', in J. Allwood and E. Hjelmquist (eds), *Foregrounding Background* (Lund, Sweden: Bokforlaget Doxa, 1985).

11. S. Garrod and A.J. Sanford, 'Topic-dependent effects in language processing', in G.B. Flores d'Arcais and R. Jarvella (eds), *Processes of Language Understanding* (Chichester: John Wiley and Sons, 1983).

12. For recent work on context-dependent speech processing in humans, see Garnham, cited in note 4. For an interesting account of a context-based artificial speech recognition system, see the description of 'HEARSAY' in D.E. Rumelhart, *Introduction to Human Information Processing* (New York: John Wiley and Sons, 1977). A source account of this system is given in D.R. Reddy, L.D. Erman, R.D. Fennell and R.B. Neely, 'The HEARSAY speech understanding system: an example of the recognition process', in *Proceedings of the Third International Joint Conference on Artificial Intelligence* (Stanford, California, 1973).

13. Quite obviously, there are some aspects of 'how to ride a bike' which can be put into words. But it is notoriously difficult to describe in any detail at all. In contrast, 'how to stop a bus' can be described satisfactorily. However, it is all a matter of degree. Stopping a bus involves arm movements and bodily orientations which one could not possibly describe.

14. Stereotyped event sequences are a large part of our cultural heritage. When in France, it is normal to have one's cheese course at dinner before one's sweet. In the UK it is the other way around. Such orderings are learned at a very early age. Many prescriptive stereotypes can be thought of as potential problems for which stereotypes provide a culturally ready-made solution.

15. R. Schank and R. Abelson, *Scripts, Goals, Plans, and Understanding: an Enquiry into Human Knowledge Structures* (Hillsdale, N.J.: Lawrence Erlbaum Associates, 1977).

16. M. Minsky, 'A framework for representing knowledge', in P.H. Winston (ed.), *The Psychology of Computer Vision* (New York: McGraw-Hill, 1975).

17. The details of matching a language input to a knowledge structure requires that they are written in mutually accessible formats. This is no problem in principle from a purely programming viewpoint, but there are many different ways of going about it. Some of these are illustrated in R.C. Schank and K.M. Colby, *Computer Models of Thought and Language* (San Francisco: Freeman, 1973). Equally interesting problems are those of how many clues are needed for a processor to accept a script as relevant. Mention of key words is not good enough. If 'cinema' were good enough, then the following would invoke a cinema script:
    Max walked past the cinema.
    This is a complex issue, and is discussed in the book by Schank and Abelson; see note 15.

18. Frame is a term which can be used to describe almost any modular datastructure having defaults. For instance, Minsky's notion ranges from 'grammar frames' which consist in default data about grammar, through to complete points of view and frames of reference in scientific thinking—so-called scientific pardigms.

19. This distinction between the necessary and the merely typical is a general definitional problem familiar to philosophers. One of the attractive features of Minsky's treatment is that it allows necessary properties where possible, typical but not necessary features to be known as such, and can code information which highlights possible failures of this sort of classification without losing value as a definitional system.

20. A full description is given in Anne Anderson, S. Garrod and A.J. Sanford, 'The accessibility of pronominal antecedents as a function of episode shifts in narrative text', *Quarterly Journal of Experimental Psychology*, **17** (1983), 427–20.

21. This is an oversimplification. The idea of 'main character' is important in the comprehension of narratives. In fact, references to main characters are usually resolved more quickly than those to secondary characters, but this complication does not seriously affect the present observations.

22. These puzzles are well known to all readers of brainteaser columns. The most interesting (and irritating) thing about them is that solving one type of pre-supposition does not make it much easier to solve another, different type.

23. See D.E. Rumelhart, *Human Information Processing* (New York: John Wiley and Sons, 1977).

24. S. Garrod and A.J. Sanford, 'On the real time character of interpretation during reading', *Language and Cognitive Processes*, **1** (1985), 43–61.

CHAPTER 3

1. D.A. Hinsley, J.R. Hayes and H.A. Simon, 'From words to equations: meaning representation in algebra word problems', in P.A. Carpenter and M. A. Just (eds), *Cognitive Processes in Comprehension* (Hillsdale, N.J.: Lawrence Erlbaum Associates, 1977). This provides a very good discussion of this and related issues.

2. E.A. Silver, 'Recall of mathematical information: solving related problems', *Journal of Research in Mathematics Education*, **12** (1981), 54–64.

3. I am not sure of the origins of this puzzle, but I am grateful to Peter Dienes who introduced it to me at an Open University summer school some years back.

4. Data taken from personal research as yet unpublished. Having tested over 50 people on this problem in different conditions, only very few people see the solution quickly.

5. It is difficult to produce an intuitively compelling proof, but the problem hinges on the constraints governing the removal of the cup in the second phase. Being wrong in the first place is the most likely event, the chances being 2/3. Thus, two-thirds of the time, there is no choice about which cup is left when one is removed. The one to which you (incorrectly) pointed cannot be removed, neither can the one which the coin is under. So the cup which is left *has to be* the one with the coin under. Since this is true on 2/3 of all occasions, *by changing your choice* you can be correct on 2/3 of all occasions. If you stick, you will only be correct on 1/3 of all occasions. Thus the odds are 2:1 in favour of changing your choice.

6. A useful discussion of various views on metaphor is A. Ortony (ed.), *Metaphor and Thought* (Cambridge: Cambridge University Press, 1979).

7. This is strictly a 'literal' statement of similarity, but serves to make the point about asymmetry.

8. G. Miller discusses the general problem of the propositional representation of similes and metaphors, and relates it to processing considerations. His paper is one of the seminal psychological papers in the field, and is found in note 6, above.

9. Sentence structure is analysed by some linguists into 'given' and 'new' components, which correspond well with psychologically motivated accounts of what people know (given) and what information they have to relate to what they know (new). The classic but difficult paper in this field is M.A.K. Halliday, 'Notes on transitivity and theme in English', *Journal of Linguistics*, **3** (1967), 37–81, 199–214.

10. See Miller, note 6.

11. The role of analogy in scientific reasoning has been indicated informally by many scientists and philosophers of science. Only recently have empirical studies been carried out on what this means. The work of Gentner and Gentner, to be described here, is seminal in this

respect: D. Gentner and D.R. Gentner, 'Flowing waters or teeming crowds: Mental models of electricity', in D. Gentner and A.L. Stevens (eds), *Mental Models* (1983). In addition to their experimental work, these authors discuss in detail the representation of the well-known solar system/atom analogy described here.

12. Description given by a psychology student invited to provide such an explanation in class.

13. From A. Beiser, *Basic Concepts of Physics* (London: Addison-Wesley Inc., 1961).

14. With series-resistors, the relationship between total resistance and individual resistances is given by R(total) = R1 + R2, where R1 and R2 are the individual values. With parallel ones, the rule is 1/R(total) = 1/R1 + 1R2. R(total) thus turns out to be smaller than R1 or R2 in the second case.

15. A number of introductory books on geology discuss the story of rift valleys. See, for example, A. Holmes, *Principles of Physical Geology* (London: Thomas Nelson and Sons, 1965).

16. H. Cloos, 'Hebung-Spattung-Vulkanismus', *Geologische Rundschan*, **30** (1939), 405–527.

17. G. Lakoff and M. Johnson, *Metaphors We Live by* (London: University of Chicago Press, 1980).

18. The potential correlation between up–down and quantity is made all the more attractive by classical work of Jean Piaget on conservation in children. Piaget observed that, at a certain stage of development, children thought that when a fixed volume of liquid was poured from a wide, low container into a tall, narrow one, so that the height of the liquid was greater, that there was 'more liquid'. Perhaps the foundations for certain metaphors lie at the very heart of our intellectual development as individuals. See J.H. Flavell, *The Developmental Psychology of Jean Piaget* (London: Van Nostrand Rheinhold, 1963).

CHAPTER 4

1. For a review of heuristics used in general problem-solving, see A. Newell and H.A. Simon *Human Problem-Solving* (Englewood Cliffs, N.J.: Prentice Hall, 1972).

2. A recent compendium of research in this area is D. Kahneman, P. Slovic and A. Tversky, *Judgement under Uncertainty: Heuristics and Biases* (Cambridge: Cambridge University Press, 1982).

3. Memory is exceptionally sensitive to the frequency of events. This seems to be an automatic process, frequency being somehow registered without one being aware of the fact. See L. Hasher and W. Chromiak, 'The processing of frequency information: An automatic mechanism?', *Journal of Verbal Learning and Verbal Behaviour*, **16** (1977), 173–84.

4. For example, see A.D. Baddeley, *The Psychology of Memory* (New York: Harper & Row, 1976).
5. Personal experiences are more vivid, probably because they are more richly represented, and because they are more likely to have emotional significance.
6. It might seem counter-intuitive that more complex memory representations result in better recall, but it is so. Human memory is not to be thought of as a mere record of data coming in from the outside world. Rather, much of what is stored in memory depends upon the input having been interpreted. Thus we find it easier to remember things which have 'meaning' than we do meaningless things. For instance, it is easier to remember a text which one understands than it is to remember one which one does not understand. The implication is that rich memory structures support the retention of new information. These points are discussed in many introductory books, for instance, A.J. Sanford, *Cognition and Cognitive Psychology* (London: Weidenfeld and Nicolson, 1985), pp. 118–57.
7. A. Tversky and D. Kahneman, 'Availability: A heuristic for judging frequency and probability', *Cognitive Psychology*, **4** (1973), 207–32.
8. M. Ross and F. Sicoly, 'Egocentricity biases in availability and attribution', *Journal of Personality and Social Psychology*, **37** (1979), 322–36.
9. This is probably related to the way in which search is to some extent based upon stem generation, as discussed in Chapter 1 in the section on anagram generation.
10. A full description of this experiment is given in the paper by Kahneman and Tversky (note 7, above). Mathematically, the maximum number of possible committees occurs when there are 5 out of 10 people to be in the committee, and is no less than 252!
11. D. Kahneman and A. Tversky 'Subjective probability: A judgement of representativeness', *Cognitive Psychology*, **3** (1972), 430–54.
12. To understand this, first note that we are talking about exact birth orders. Try listing the possible orders for five children. BBBBB, GGGGG, BBBBG, GGGGB, etc. for a while. Now each of these sequences is about equally likely, but there are far less with all boys or all girls than with one boy or one girl, and very many with two of one sex and three of the other.
13. A. Tversky and D. Kahneman (1982), Chapter 6 of the volume given in note 2.
14. Bayes theorem is described and derived in most introductory books on probability theory. See for example, W. Feller, *An Introduction to Probability Theory and its Applications* (London: John Wiley and Sons, 1968). this book also contains some descriptions of very counter-intuitive facts deriving from the logic of probability.
15. L. D. Phillips and W. Edwards, 'Conservatism in simple probability inference tasks', *Journal of Experimental Psychology*, **72** (1966), 346–57.
16. D. Kahneman and A. Tversky, 'On the psychology of prediction', *Psychological Review*, **80** (1973), 237–51.

17. M. Hammerton, 'A case of radical probability estimation', *Journal of Experimental Psychology*, **101** (1973) 252–4.

18. Apart from the literature on probability combination, base-rate problems are well known in social psychology, as we shall see in Chapter 6.

19. Tversky and Kahneman (1982), Chapter 8 of the volume given in note 2.

20. H.P. Weld and M. Roff, 'A study in the formation of opinion based upon legal evidence', *Journal of Psychology*, **51** (1938), 609–28.

21. For a general review of the calibration problem, see S. Lichtenstein, B. Fischhoff and L.D. Phillips, Chapter 22, in the work described in note 2.

22. A. Koriat, S. Lichtenstein and B. Fischhoff 'Reasons for confidence', *Journal of Experimental Psychology: Human Perception and Performance*, **1** (1980), 288–99.

23. e.g. B. Fischhoff, 'Hindsight ≠ Foresight: The effect of outcome knowledge on judgement under uncertainty', *Journal of Experimental Psychology: Human Perception and Performance*, **1** (1975), 288–99.

24. P. Slovic and B. Fischhoff, 'On the psychology of experimental surprises', *Journal of Experimental Psychology: Human Perception and Performance*, **3** (1977), 544–51.

25. For an entertaining review, see B. Fischhoff, 'For those condemned to study the past: Heuristics and biases in hindsight', Chapter 23 in the work given in note 2.

26. See, for example, W.C. Ward and H.M. Jenkins, 'The display of information and the judgement of contingency', *Canadian Journal of Psychology*, **19** (1965), 231–41.

27. P. C. Wason, 'Reasoning about a rule', *Quarterly Journal of Experimental Psychology*, **20** (1968), 273–81. Also see P.C. Wason, 'On the Failure to Eliminate Hypotheses . . . A second look', in P.N. Johnson-Laird and P.C. Wason (eds), *Thinking: Readings in Cognitive Science* (Cambridge: Cambridge University Press, 1977).

28. C.R. Mynatt, M.E. Doherty and R.D. Tweney 'Confirmation bias in a simulated research environment: An experimental study of scientific inference', *Quarterly Journal of Experimental Psychology*, **29** (1977), 85–95.

29. H.J. Einhorn, 'Learning from experience and suboptimal rules in decision-making', in T.S. Wallsten (ed.), *Cognitive Processes in Choice and Decision Behavior* (Hillsdale, N.J.: Lawrence Erlbaum Associates, 1980).

CHAPTER 5

1. L.J. Rips and S.L. Marcus, 'Supposition and the analysis of conditional sentences', in M.A. Just and P.A. Carpenter (eds), *Cognitive Processes in Comprehension* (Hillsdale, N.J.: Lawrence Erlbaum Associates, 1977).

2. H. Markovits, 'Awareness of the "possible" as a mediator of formal thinking in conditional reasoning problems', *British Journal of Psychology*, **75** (1984), 367–76.

3. See P.C. Wason and P.N. Johnson-Laird, *Psychology of Reasoning: Structure and content* (Cambridge, Mass.: Harvard University Press, 1972).

4. P.N. Johnson-Laird, P. Legrenzi and M.S. Legrenzi, 'Reasoning and sense of reality', *British Journal of Psychology*, **63** (1972), 396–400.

5. For a classic account of the confirmation bias, see P.C. Wason 'Reasoning about a rule', *Quarterly Journal of Experimental Psychology*, **52** (1968), 133–42.

6. From K.I. Manktelow and J. St B. Evans, 'Facilitation of reasoning by realism: Effect or non-effect?', *British Journal of Psychology*, **70** (1979), 477–88.

7. J.R. Cox and R.A. Griggs, 'The effects of experience on performance in Wason's selection task', *Memory and Cognition*, **10** (1982), 496–502.

8. P.N. Johnson-Laird, *Mental Models* (Cambridge: Cambridge University Press, 1983).

9. The term 'quantity expression' is used to distinguish natural language expressions from logical quantifiers.

10. Better-known systems of 'representing' the information given in syllogisms are Euler's circles and Venn diagrams. The advantage of Johnson-Laird's system is that it is easy to understand at a glance, and corresponds more closely to psychologically plausible representations.

11. Unpublished thesis research by L. Moxey at the Glasgow Psychology Department shows how with certain quantity expressions one or other aspect of the set of people can be emphasised.

12. e.g. M. Wilkins, 'The effect of changed material on ability to do formal syllogistic reasoning', *Archives of Psychology*, **16** (1928), 83. See also I. Jarvis and P. Frick, 'The relationship between attitudes toward conclusions and errors in judging logical validity of syllogisms', *Journal of Experimental Psychology*, **33** (1943), 73–7.

13. J. St B. Evans, J. Barston and P. Pollard, 'On the conflect between logic and belief in syllogistic reasoning', *Memory and Cognition*, **11** (1983), 295–306.

14. J.V. Oakhill and P.N. Johnson-Laird, 'The effects of belief on the spontaneous production of syllogistic conclusions', *Quarterly Journal of Experimental Psychology*, **37A** (1985), 553–69.

15. B. Russell, *Mysticism and Logic* (London: George Allen and Unwin, 1929).

CHAPTER 6

1. F. Heider, *The Psychology of Interpersonal Relations* (New York: John Wiley and Sons, 1958).

2. It must be understood that the account given in this chapter is very limited, and that even major orientations have been omitted. The purpose is to indicate a potential continuity between non-social reasoning and social judgement.

3. This perspective, called the hermeneutic perspective, is now being used by many workers in an attempt to review the entire foundation of work on attribution. See especially W. Turnbull, 'Everyday explanation: The pragmatics of puzzle resolution', *Journal for the Theory of Social Behaviour*, in press.

4. An example of this is the 'self-centred' bias in assuming responsibility for joint enterprises, as discussed in Chapter 4 (cf. note 8 of that chapter).

5. J.S. Mill, *System of Logic* (London: J.W. Parker, 1851).

6. H.L.H. Hart and A.M.Honoré, *Causation and the Law* (Oxford: Clarendon Press 1959).

7. D.J. Hilton and B.R. Slugoski, 'Knowledge-based causal attribution: The "abnormal conditons focus" model', *Psychological Review*, in press.

8. D. Kahneman and A. Tversky, 'The simulation heuristic', in D. Kahneman, P. Slovic and A. Tversky, *Judgement under Uncertainty: Heuristics and Biases* (Cambridge: Cambridge University Press, 1982).

9. It has been supposed by many social psychologists that the internal (person) and external (circumstance) categories are central to human reasoning, and that the three dimensions of information to be described provide mutually exclusive categories enabling attributions to be made. This point of view is not without its critics.

10. H.H. Kelley, 'Attribution in social psychology', *Nebraska Symposium on Motivation*, **15** (1967), 192–238.

11. J.L. Mackie, *The Cement of the Universe* (London: Oxford University Press, 1974).

12. L.Z. McArthur, 'The how and what of why: Some determinants of causal attribution', *Journal of Personality and Social Psychology*, **22** (1972), 171–93.

13. J.M.F. Jaspers, M.R.C. Hewstone, and F.D. Fincham, 'Attribution theory and research: The state of the art', J.M.F. Jaspers, F.D. Fincham and M.R.C. Hewstone (eds), *Attribution Theory: Essays and Experiments* (London: Academic Press, 1983).

14. It is not possible to do justice to Hilton and Slugoski's work here, even to the extent of describing their experimental work in much detail, since a full specification of abnormal conditions would require a large number of illustrations.

15. L. Ross 'The intuitive psychologist and his shortcomings: Distortions in the attribution process', in L. Berkowitz (ed.), *Advances in Experimental Social Psychology*, vol. 10 (New York: Academic Press, 1977).

16. L. Ross, T. Amabile and J. Steinmets, 'Social roles, social control, and biases in social perception processes', *Journal of Personality and Social Psychology*, **35** (1977), 485–94.

17. R.E. Nisbett, G.C. Caputo, P. Legant and J. Mereck, 'Behaviour as seen by the actor and the observer', *Journal of Personality and Social Psychology*, **27** (1973), 154–64.
18. E.E. Jones and R.E. Nisbett, 'The actor and the observer: Divergent perceptions of the causes of behaviour', in E.E. Jones, D.E. Kanouse, H.H. Kelley, R.E. Nisbett, S. Valins and B. Weiner (eds), *Attribution: Perceiving the Causes of Behavior* (Morristown, N.J.: General Learning Press, 1972).
19. For example, S.E. Taylor and J.H. Koivumaki, 'The perception of self and others: Acquaintanceship, affect and actor–observer differences', *Journal of Personality and Social Psychology*, **33** (1976), 403–8.
20. The view favoured by Jones and Nisbett, cited in note 18.
21. For an accessible review, see Chapter 7 of S.T. Friske and S.E. Taylor, *Social Cognition* (Reading, Mass.: Addison-Wesley Publishing Co.).
22. S. Duval and R.A. Wicklund, *A Theory of Objective Self-awareness* (New York: Academic Press, 1972).
23. For example, R. Nisbett and L. Ross, *Human Inference: Strategies and Shortcomings* (Englewood Cliffs, N.J.: Prentice-Hall, 1980). This book is a fascinating study of bias in human inference-making (especially social aspects), including work on availability and representativeness. The volume by Kahneman, Slovic and Tversky (Chapter 4, note 2) also contains much relevant material and comment.

CHAPTER 7

1. E.G.A. Barr and E.A. Feigenbaum (eds), *The Handbook of Artificial Intelligence*, Vol. 2 (Los Altos, California: William Kaufman, 1982).
2. S.J. Kaplan, 'Cooperative responses from a portable natural language database query system', in M. Brady and R. Berwick (eds), *Computational Models of Discourse* (Cambridge, Mass.: MIT Press, 1983).
3. This particular experiment, and related problems of understanding motion, are discussed in M. McCloskey, 'Naive theories of motion', in D. Gentner and A.L. Stevens (eds), *Mental Models* (Hillsdale, N.J.: Lawrence Erlbaum Associates, 1983).
4. In addition to note 3, see also J. Clement, 'Students' preconceptions in introductory mechanics', *American Journal of Physics*, **50** (1982), 66–71.
5. A.A. di Sessa (1983), 'Phenomenology and the evolution of intuition', in Gentner and Stevens (see note 3).
6. R. H. Thouless, *Straight and Crooked Thinking* (London: Hodder and Stoughton, 1930).

INDEX

Index

DATE DUE
